Capacity: The New Advantage

Achieve Greater Productivity
Without Compromising

HILANI ELLIS

Capacity: The New Advantage

Achieve Greater Productivity Without Compromising

Copyright © 2025 by Hilani Ellis

All rights reserved.

ISBN 979-8-9928280-0-9 (hardcover)
ISBN 979-8-9928280-1-6 (paperback)
eBook 979-8-9928280-2-3

Library of Congress Cataloging
LCCN: 2025904815 (print)

Cover Design: Greg Jesse

Printed in the United States of America

First Edition.

No portion of this publication may be reproduced in any form without written permission from the author, except as permitted by U.S. copyright law.

For permission requests, please contact:

www.HilaniEllis.com

What is ca·pac·i·ty?
....
kə-ˈpa-sə-tē

At its core, capacity is the ability to hold, produce, or accomplish something. It's the space we have—mentally, emotionally, and physically—to take on tasks, execute, and create meaningful outcomes.[1]

In business and leadership, capacity goes beyond mere capability. It's not just about what you can do, but how effectively you can allocate your energy, resources, and focus to achieve greater results without unnecessary strain.

A capacity mindset challenges the traditional obsession with time. While time is fixed, your capacity is flexible. By shifting your focus to capacity, you open the door to:

Creating impact - Capacity focuses on quality of effort, not just quantity of hours.

Expanding what's possible - Capacity grows when aligned with clear priorities and efficient execution.

Sustaining effort - Capacity thrives when energy is optimized, not depleted.

Before diving into this book, take a moment to consider: how would shifting to a capacity mindset reshape your ability to lead, execute, and thrive?

A Personal Thank You Note

(60-seconds)

CONTENTS

	Note to Reader	i
1	Bending Time	1
2	Decision Fatigue	20
3	Status Quo	38
4	Risk Reward	52
5	Change Capacity	65
6	Conditioning	78
7	Work-Life Harmony	95
8	The Dash	112
	Notes	119
	Acknowledgement	125
	About Author	126

NOTE TO READER

Dear Reader:

Have you ever felt like there's never enough time to get everything done, no matter how hard you try? Or wondered why the call to "work smarter, not harder" feels more urgent than ever? Having worked directly with over 400 leaders, from start-ups to large enterprises, I can confidently say these thoughts are more common than you might think. They reflect a pressing struggle shared by many navigating today's fast-paced world. ***But here's the good news: the struggle doesn't have to be permanent.*** In this book, we'll shift the focus away from time—a fixed and finite resource—and instead zero in on capacity, which is flexible, expansive, and within your control. This isn't just a change in mindset; it's an evolution in how you execute and lead.

This book is your companion on that journey. It's packed with practical strategies, real-life stories, and thought-provoking exercises designed to address productivity and leadership head-on. Each chapter offers a fresh perspective on how to maximize your capacity, prioritize effectively, and create meaningful impact—not just in your work, but in your life.

Think of these pages as an invitation. An invitation to pause, reflect, and disrupt old habits that were built for a different era. An invitation to expand your capacity, not only to achieve more but to lead with intention and inspire those around you to do the same. And most importantly, an invitation to build a legacy that feels both impactful and deeply fulfilling.

I know your time and capacity are precious. It would be

irresponsible of me to deplete either with a book that feels like a chore. That's why every chapter was crafted with intention—to energize and positively challenge you, not overwhelm you.

So, as you turn the page, consider how small adjustments in your approach could lead to a significant shift in what you achieve and how you feel. Let these pages guide your journey, uncovering the tools and insights you need to reclaim your time and focus on your capacity, so you can craft a leadership style that resonates with who you are—and where you want to go.

Exceptionally yours,
Hilani Ellis, the Capacity Architect

BENDING TIME

Each day, the secondhand ticks forward, pulling you into the future without your permission. You find yourself struggling to keep pace, often uttering the all-too-familiar words, *"I don't have time for that."* I know I'm not alone when I confess to thinking and saying these words, feeling the heavy weight of their truth. But these words are more than just a statement—they're a reflection of mounting responsibilities and a frustration at the passage of time. They reveal a battle we all face: keeping up with the relentless demands of work and life.

In some moments, this battle feels almost winnable; you have a steady grip, and time seems to bend to your will. But in other moments, it feels like time is slipping through your fingers, no matter how hard you try to hold on. The truth is, while time itself remains constant, our perception of it—and how we handle it—constantly shifts.

This chapter sets the stage for a fresh perspective on time. It's not about squeezing more into your day, but about changing how you *view* and *engage* with time altogether. Through the stories and strategies shared here, you'll begin to see how adopting a capacity-focused approach can help you bend time and achieve greater productivity without compromising.

Moving Through Time

Between the bookends of your day, work and life often feel all-consuming. For some, each passing hour brings an endless list of pressing demands—rushing from one meeting to another, answering countless emails, and multitasking. For others, the pace may not feel as overwhelming, but the weight of expectations still lingers. Regardless of intensity, this cycle of constant activity rarely allows time to reflect, strategize, or engage *deeply* with work or colleagues, and while it might appear productive, the quality of contributions and connections may suffer. This approach models a time-scarcity (i.e., reactive) work style, unintentionally promoting the wrong productivity work style, fostering an environment where the pressure to work harder becomes the norm—leading to unnecessary fatigue, diminished productivity, and high turnover. The alternative, a time-abundance (i.e., proactive) work style, shifts the focus from constant activity to meaningful execution—where strategy, capacity, and prioritization create a more effective and sustainable work style.

Yet, despite the clear benefits of embracing a time-abundance work style, today's fast-paced work environment makes it feel almost unattainable, reinforcing a time-scarcity work style as the default. The pressure to keep up often leads organizations to equate high volume and rapid execution with strong leadership and progress, creating the illusion that constant hustling signals significance and productivity. But this is a misconception—significance is not always synonymous with success. While urgency and effort have their place, greater productivity isn't about simply keeping up—it's about shaping work in a way that creates sustainable capacity and progress.

The first step in breaking free from a reactive work style—so you can experience productivity with greater ease and effectiveness—requires a conscious shift: swapping a time perception of scarcity (i.e., there isn't enough time) for one of abundance (i.e., there is enough time). This shift enables executives to prioritize meaningful efforts over sheer volume and speed, ultimately favoring impactful contributions over nonstop activity. For example, scheduling fewer but more focused and strategic meetings creates the space for deep work and thoughtful planning, enabling executives to make more intentional decisions and stronger team alignment. Working proactively not only reduces stress but also expands overall capacity.

Making this shift isn't just about working differently—it's about remodeling how we *engage* with time. As we explore our perception of time, you'll see practical ways to remodel your approach so you can step into a more effective, capacity-focused work style.

Our Perception of Time

The way we experience time isn't as fixed as we may assume—it's shaped by perception, not just the ticking of the clock. When we understand this, we gain greater influence over how we engage with time, ensuring it works for us rather than against us.

Our perception of time stems from the brain's way of processing it. When you're deeply immersed in an activity that interests you—like a creative project or a stimulating conversation—you may lose track of time, experiencing a state often referred to as "flow," where past, present, and future blur, and time seems to pass in sync with the second hand.

Conversely, when you're engaged in a mundane or stressful task, time can feel painfully slow. Imagine being trapped in an elevator for 15 minutes. Each second stretches, your heart pounds, and the silence amplifies negative emotions. Your brain fixates on the discomfort, making time feel like it's dragging. At work, the same effect happens in a disengaging meeting or when a task is of low interest—you check the clock repeatedly, restless and impatient, as minutes seem to move at a snail's pace.

This discrepancy in time perception is driven by our emotional state and level of interest—what's known as the time-emotion paradox.[1] Understanding and leveraging this paradox allows you to manage your time, focus, and capacity with greater clarity, creating a more sustainable and fulfilling work cadence.

With this in mind, let's discover how time and emotion affect how we engage with time and how it shapes productivity and outcomes.

Time-Scarcity Characteristics

Urgency - A persistent sense of pressure to complete tasks quickly and make fast decisions, often leading to a reactive work style.

Stress - A feeling of heightened pressure due to a perceived lack of time to accomplish tasks.

Micromanagement - A tendency to pay too much attention to tasks and processes to ensure they are completed on time.

Incomplete and assumption-based communication - Sharing information in a hurried manner, leaving out important details or failing to clarify key points. This can lead to misunderstandings and confusion among team members.

Time-Scarcity and Productivity

As outlined above, time-scarcity characteristics can have a negative effect on capacity, productivity, and decision making. We'll explore more about decision making and capacity in Chapter 2. When time is perceived as scarce, the pressure to accomplish work within constrained timelines intensifies. Under such conditions, it's common to rely on shortcuts rather than engage in thorough deliberation. These shortcuts may seem like a productive way of working, but they often create more inefficiencies, adding friction rather than momentum.

Shortcuts in a time-scarce work environment can take many forms: making quick decisions based on limited information, skimming emails instead of reading them fully, quick communication, or relying on assumptions rather than verification. While these habits may create the illusion of being productive, they often lead to undermining effectiveness and outcomes.

Utilizing shortcuts reminds me of a time when I was working with a new CEO, whom we'll call Stephen. He was in his first year after acquiring a healthcare business and had ambitious plans to scale it across multiple states. When he stepped in, the company had fewer than 100 employees, and while he had the vision, the reality of running a business was proving far more overwhelming than he had anticipated.

Stephen's background in private equity was extensive—he had spent years orchestrating high-stakes, large-scale transactions, where speed and responsiveness determined success. Yet, stepping into the role of CEO for the first time presented an entirely new set of demands and challenges. While his experience gave him a strategic advantage, he vastly underestimated the daily operational demands of running a company—an area he had little interest in.

The pressure was relentless. He found himself working long hours, bouncing between meetings, hiring decisions, and dealing with day-to-day administrative fires. To keep up, he resorted to shortcuts—skimming emails instead of reading them, making snap decisions based on gut instinct rather than analysis, and running late to meetings. Communication was often rushed, and details were missed. His approach was unsustainable.

During a meeting about building out his executive team, I asked him how he managed his time—specifically, his schedule. Without hesitation, he replied, "I wait for someone to text me asking where I am, and then I know I'm supposed to be somewhere."

My jaw practically hit the floor. This wasn't just a shortcut—respectfully, it was chaos. His avoidance of actively managing his schedule reflected a poor relationship with time and led to suboptimal choices and mounting inefficiencies, impacting his effectiveness as a leader.

This lack of structure didn't just affect him—it rippled across his organization. Team members were required to live in a reactive state, unsure of priorities or next steps. Progress was impacted, and the lack of coordination bred frustration and wasted effort. Sadly, his shortcuts were slowing team momentum, creating a culture of scrambling instead of strategizing.

However, after we worked together to onboard a new executive team member, his work style shifted significantly. With someone positioned to focus on daily operations, he earned back much needed capacity to focus on his vision, employees, and key priorities.

Stephen's story is a common example of how a time-scarce, reactive work style can cripple even the most qualified individuals, highlighting the critical need for better time perception. In contrast, let's explore a time-abundance approach.

Time-Abundance Characteristics

Strategic thinking - Prioritizing planning, allocating time for reflection, analysis, and long-term goal setting.

Innovation - Viewing time as a resource for creativity, exploring new ideas and approaches to enhance productivity and collaboration.

Delegation - Handing off tasks effectively, transferring knowledge, trusting team members to deliver so an executive can focus on higher-level responsibilities.

Clarity and thoughtfulness - Prioritizing concise communication and taking time to articulate ideas, goals, and expectations in a way that the team and stakeholders can easily understand. This helps prevent misunderstandings, promoting alignment.

Time-Abundance and Productivity

When we embrace a time-abundance mindset, we approach our role with a fundamentally different perspective than someone gripped by time-scarcity. Instead of viewing time as a finite resource to be rationed and guarded, it is perceived as abundant and flexible. This mindset lets an executive prioritize strategic thinking, long-term planning, creating a culture of creativity and innovation within an organization. Because a time-abundance executive believes there's enough time to meet demands and discover upsides, they are less likely to succumb to the pressures of urgency that leads to suboptimal choices and outcomes.

With a time-abundance mindset, an executive is able to exude a calmer disposition. They understand that managing their own time and that of their team—through the lens of time abundance and capacity preservation—is crucial for sustained performance and effectiveness. This approach fosters purposeful delegation, enabling executives to collaborate with their team while reserving their capacity for high-level strategic initiatives. And, because time is in their favor, if further communication is needed, they are open and ready to engage. By fostering a work environment where time is viewed as an abundant resource rather than an adversary, executives cultivate a culture of productivity and continuous momentum.

Having worked with several hundred executives, I've found that about thirty percent exhibit a time-abundance work style. One CEO in particular, from a private equity firm—we'll call her Julie—comes to mind. During an onboarding session I facilitated between her and her new executive team member, I emphasized the importance of managing her energy (capacity) first, then her time. I introduced the concept of the *power* of 60 seconds (more on this in a moment) and encouraged her to view each day as a new opportunity to transfer knowledge, rather than simply another day in the role. I stressed that leveraging 60 seconds as a resource would pay off tremendously, fostering the optimal work cadence she and her new team member craved.

At the end of the session, Julie offered her new team member this insightful guidance: "I'm fully aware of my speed. I've been operating like this for years. You have full permission to tell me when I'm moving too quickly. At times, I may sound frustrated because you're asking me to slow down, but I know the goal is to help you keep pace and eventually, position yourself ahead of me."

This feedback showed not only Julie's awareness of her own work style but also her willingness to adapt for the benefit of her new team member. That awareness reinforces a culture capable of navigating change and uncertainty, strengthening the team's overall change capacity. We'll talk more about change capacity in Chapter 5.

Instead of viewing unexpected disruptions as obstacles, executives can look at them as opportunities for growth and adaptation. This flexibility lets executives leverage time as a tool for greater productivity. Furthermore, by embodying a time-abundance mindset, executives can inspire their teams to achieve demands and ambitious goals sustainably.

The Power of 60 Seconds

Imagine if I asked you to put down this book and find an open space on the floor where you could assume and maintain (if you are able) a plank position for one minute (60 seconds). While holding the plank and having a conversation, could you accurately estimate when 60 seconds had lapsed? Most people tend to ask, "How much longer?" around the 27-second mark, which is less than half of the total time. The same 60 seconds that feel effortless in a casual conversation suddenly stretch when paired with discomfort. This contrast highlights how our perception of time isn't fixed—it's shaped by external conditions, mental engagement, and even physical strain. The time-emotion paradox is present in this example.

You might have noticed I wrote both *one minute* and *60 seconds.* This is the foundation of the 60-Second Rule: while they represent the same amount of time, the way we frame it can influence how we perceive it. Like Julie's story, I regularly advised leaders to reframe *one minute* as *60 seconds,* leveraging the larger number to foster a perception of greater time availability and control. By simply changing the language, we create a subtle but powerful shift in how we approach demands, helping to manage pressure and maintain capacity.

Time perception isn't just about how we measure it—it's also about how we use it. Take speech, for example: clear, intentional communication averages around 100 words per 60 seconds, while casual conversation can reach 200. The difference is significant. Leaders who understand how speech cadence shapes productivity know when to slow down to improve clarity or pick up the pace to drive momentum. This ability to adjust, based on what the moment demands, creates a strategic advantage in communication.[2]

To illustrate the 60-Second Rule for time perception and individual communication styles, imagine this scenario: someone on your team processes information slower than you, resulting in a slow verbal cadence. Each question you pose is met with a prolonged pause, as your team member carefully considers their response. If you're a quick executive who thrives on quick exchanges and rapid decision making, you might find yourself growing impatient during these interactions. As you wait, the seconds tick by and you can feel your own sense of urgency rising. You might start to fidget, glance at your phone, or even interrupt to fill the silence, hoping to speed up the conversation. These reactions not only create a tense atmosphere, but also risk shutting down valuable input from the team member. Their thoughtful, deliberate response could provide crucial insights or innovative solutions, but rushing to move forward—versus quietly counting down 60 seconds to lend time for reflection—might cause you to miss their contribution. Remember the example of holding a 60-second plank? The duration is longer than we realize.

Over time, this dynamic can lead to productivity challenges. When speed is consistently prioritized over thoughtful deliberation, team members—regardless of their natural communication pace—may adjust their approach to match the prevailing urgency, sometimes at the cost of clarity or depth. Those who process information more deliberately might hesitate to share insights, concerned that their approach is seen as inefficient. Meanwhile, those who naturally communicate quickly may feel compelled to respond even faster, potentially leading to surface-level discussions rather than well-rounded ones. Additionally, other team members may observe these patterns and mirror the behavior, reinforcing a time-scare, reactive culture where quickness overshadows strategic progress.

For executives, recognizing and addressing this dynamic is vital. By acknowledging the true passage of time, different processing speeds, and communication styles within a team, executives can create an environment where everyone engages and communicates in a way that's comfortable for them. It starts with something as familiar as the phrase, "Got a minute?"—a question we've all heard or said. But how often does that minute actually last just 60 seconds? More often than not, it stretches into five or ten. This subtle disconnect between the ask and the reality highlights the importance of setting clearer expectations around time and attention. When leaders model intentionality around brief exchanges—whether using the 60-Second Rule, a 120-second check-in, or simply naming the purpose upfront—they encourage the same respect for time across the team.

Let's explore two different scenarios to see the rule in action. Context for this scenario: the CFO has been with the company for six months. The VP of Finance has been with the company for three years. They have implemented across the organization the 60-Second Rule to promote clarity and effectiveness during communication.

CFO: "Got 60 seconds?"

VP of Finance: "Sure."

CFO: "I noticed some discrepancies in the Q1 report. Can you clarify?"

VP of Finance: "Certainly. Do you have a specific section in mind?"

CFO: "Yes, the expenditure breakdown on page three. The numbers don't seem to match our projections, particularly in the technology investments line."

VP of Finance: "The variance is due to a recent investment in new technology. We accelerated the purchase of upgraded software and hardware to support our upcoming projects and improve operational efficiency. These were anticipated costs, but they were realized earlier than expected."

CFO: "So, the higher costs are a strategic move to enhance our infrastructure. Are there any other unexpected expenses we should be aware of?"

BENDING TIME

VP of Finance: "At this time, no other significant expenses. The rest of the expenditures are within the projected range. We should see the benefits of this investment starting to reflect in our productivity metrics by the end of Q2."

CFO: "Thanks for the insight. It's reassuring to know these costs were planned and beneficial. Let's monitor the impact closely and adjust our forecasts accordingly for Q2."

VP of Finance: "Absolutely. I'll prepare a brief on the expected ROI and keep the team updated on the progress."

In roughly 60 seconds, clarity was gained on an issue. By adopting the 60-Second Rule, the coworkers used a small amount of time to ensure transparency and mutual understanding. Specificity of communication helps strengthen outcomes. Using a time-abundance perspective during activities and conversations improves efficiency and engagement. As Benjamin Franklin once said, "For every minute spent organizing, an hour is earned."[3]

Now, consider this example of a 60-second duration to help navigate a stressful situation. Imagine that you're a CEO preparing to address your company's annual shareholders' meeting. With 20 minutes left before you step onto the stage, you notice tension and uncertainty among your executive team regarding a key strategic decision. Sensing the urgency, you call for a 60-second silence exercise. You ask each member to jot down their top two concerns and propose solution(s) on sticky notes.

During this brief pause, the energy in the room shifts from anxious anticipation to focused reflection. As the seconds tick by, minds sharpen. The exercise allows each executive to organize their thoughts while fostering a collective sense of clarity and purpose.

After the 60 seconds are up, you use the remaining time to discuss insights. Sticky notes and concise exchanges quickly lead to alignment. The team emerges with a unified strategy and renewed energy. This moment demonstrates how a brief pause can transform uncertainty into decisive action, enhancing the team's collective capacity (energy). This moment reinforces an essential truth: time isn't the only factor at play—how we manage and direct our capacity determines the clarity, momentum, and impact of our efforts.

Capacity-Focused Work Style

Bending time isn't about manipulating the clock—it's about shifting focus from managing it to optimizing and capitalizing on your capacity, which is fueled by how you structure your work and manage your energy.

Capacity and energy are deeply intertwined—when energy is depleted, capacity shrinks; when energy is managed intentionally, capacity expands. Consider two executives tackling the same high-priority task. One, drained from back-to-back meetings, struggles to think clearly and takes twice as long to complete the work. The other, having structured their day with capacity in mind, approaches the task with greater focus, completing it in less time. Both have the same hours, but their ability to execute is vastly different.

As illustrated, capacity isn't just about available time—it's about how energy fuels execution. When executives intentionally manage and protect their capacity, they create a new advantage—one that allows them to consistently perform at a higher level, without relying on unsustainable hustle.

To sustain that advantage, executives need to move beyond

simply managing tasks and schedules and start organizing their work through the lens of capacity and strategic importance. This capacity-focused mindset helps executives bend time in a way that prioritizes both performance and longevity—because not all activities contribute equally to long-term outcomes.

This is where Return on Capacity (ROC) comes into play. When leaders evaluate work based on how much it drains or fuels their capacity, they gain a clearer understanding of which efforts deliver the greatest value. Some demands—often non-negotiable—will naturally draw on capacity, but being intentional about balancing these with work that replenishes it ensures executives can sustain both their performance and productivity.

By recognizing which activities fuel capacity and which deplete it, executives can make more intentional decisions about where to invest their time and energy. This capacity awareness allows them to adjust their approach in real-time, preserving capacity for the work that delivers the greatest outcomes. But capacity isn't limitless—and when mismanaged, it comes at a cost. This capacity cost—the hidden trade-offs of where and how energy is spent—will be explored further in Chapter 6.

Using a capacity-focused work style offers many benefits, particularly when it comes to team cohesion. By combining a focus on capacity with one of time-abundance, executives ensure they have the right resources to encourage, support, and engage with their team members in meaningful ways. Doing this fosters a collaborative and supportive work environment where team members feel integral to the mission. As a result, companies build stronger teams, creating a more cohesive rhythm, generating sustainable momentum.

CAPACITY: THE NEW ADVANTAGE

A capacity-focused work style isn't just about creating efficiency—it's about elevating one's leadership style. Your leadership style is the perception others have of your character, values, and effectiveness. This is often referred to as one's personal brand—a concept we'll explore further in the final chapter. One client who exemplified this shift—focusing on return on capacity for both him and his team—was a managing partner at a top law firm, whom we'll call Sean. Our collaboration focused on building out his leadership team, and during one of our discussions, I asked him about a personal development goal he was working on. Without hesitation, Sean responded, "I'm being more intentional in my one-on-one meetings. I'm focusing on listening more rather than talking."

Sean elaborated on his journey to becoming a more attentive leader. He realized that his natural inclination to exude dominant, rushed energy during conversations often left his team members feeling overlooked. Determined to correct this, Sean began practicing mindful listening. (Sidebar: I often disrupt the term 'active listening' with 'mindful listening', because 'active' to me means busy, and when used in this way, it could convey that your mind is busy while listening.) Sean made a conscious effort to give his full attention during meetings, resisting deep-rooted energy habits to interrupt or immediately offer solutions. He shared that it wasn't easy, but gradually, he began to notice the positive return from his remodeling efforts. His investment in remodeling the underserving habits required constant conditioning—a concept we'll explore further in Chapter 6.

By intentionally focusing on his capacity and that of his team, Sean was building a culture of collaboration and mutual respect with his coworkers. This intentionality in his one-on-one interactions significantly elevated his leadership style, positioning him as a thoughtful and engaging leader dedicated to the success of his team.

Remodeling Your Leadership Work Style

Throughout this chapter, I've shared strategies designed to help you bend your perception of time and demonstrated how small shifts in your approach can naturally expand your capacity, elevating your productivity and leadership brand. Each story and insight introduced practical, easy-to-implement techniques—allowing you to begin remodeling your work style without adding unnecessary strain.

When leaders appear constantly overwhelmed or rushed, it signals—whether intentional or not—that they lack control over their time. This perception doesn't just impact their own effectiveness; it diminishes confidence across the team, stifles collaboration, and slows progress. Leaders who are gripped by time instead of commanding their capacity risk losing both influence and trust.

On the other hand, when your team experiences you as present, focused, and available to engage, it opens new levels of productivity, creativity, and alignment—fueling both individual and collective capacity.

Adopting even one of the strategies from this chapter can start the remodeling process, giving you the tools to adjust your work style, amplify your capacity, and cultivate a leadership presence that encourages and drives sustainable progress. Your leadership brand isn't just about what you accomplish; it's about how you show up—and your capacity is the foundation that allows it to thrive.

CAPACITY: THE NEW ADVANTAGE

"Capacity currency is the new wealth." - Hilani Ellis

Self-Assessment

Answer yes or no to each question.

1. Do you frequently feel rushed or pressured by deadlines?
2. Do you attempt to multitask to save time?
3. Do you set aside specific times for focused work without interruptions?
4. Do you have a system to prioritize your tasks each day?
5. Do you take regular breaks to recharge throughout the day?
6. Do you prioritize tasks based on your peak energy levels rather than just the clock?
7. Do you regularly delegate tasks to ensure that you're focusing your capacity on high-impact activities?

Scoring and Guidance

More yes answers: You may have a time-abundance relationship with time. Consider strategies to manage your energy and focus on high-priority tasks.

More no answers: You likely have a time-scarcity relationship with time. Continue refining your time and capacity management practices for optimal productivity.

Launch Pad

1. **Partner with a team member:** Choose someone on your team and introduce the 60-Second Rule (or extend it to 120 seconds if needed). Explain how the rule supports adopting a time-abundance mindset and creates space for more

thoughtful communication. Encourage them—like in Julie's story—to call out when old habits surface, reinforcing the remodeling process and building accountability.

2. **Announce at your next meeting:** Formally introduce the rule of taking an additional 60 seconds to reflect, discuss and/or confirm objectives and next steps. Champion the importance of this practice for improving clarity, alignment, and capacity preservation.

3. **Shift the focus:** Start actively telling those you engage with, *"I'm shifting my focus from time to the ROC—considering what a [specific task or project] truly needs from me and my team."* This shift in language reinforces the importance of capacity focus over clock-watching. Over time, it not only shapes how others view your leadership but also helps elevate your organization's productivity culture.

DECISION FATIGUE

How many decisions do you think a person makes in a single day? Research suggests that an adult makes around 35,000 conscious decisions daily—from major ones that shape business outcomes to trivial choices like what to eat.[1] During my research, I came across a fascinating Cornell study revealing that out of the thousands of decisions we make daily, 200 are focused solely on food.[2] It's not surprising when you think about it. Even something as simple as ordering lunch can drain your mental capacity. Do you want a salad? If yes, which one? Or maybe a burger? If so, should you add cheese? The endless array of choices forces your brain to work harder, gradually depleting your capacity. And if you're hangry (i.e., irritable because of hunger), it's even more draining; you don't want to think about it, you just want to eat.

The Cornell study reminded me of a time when I was presenting to a group of fifteen CEOs. When asked what they'd like to eliminate from their daily routine to reduce decision fatigue, one CEO responded candidly, "I wish I didn't have to stop and eat. I waste precious time trying to decide what to eat and consuming the meal." The room was filled with understanding nods. The CEO's frustration underscores how decision fatigue isn't confined to complex, work-related tasks but includes even simple, trivial tasks.

Now, imagine combining many simple, yet capacity-draining activities with a demanding to-do list and a back-to-back schedule—it's no wonder even the most driven executives experience decision fatigue. When fatigue sets in, executives often fall into reactive cycles, prioritizing quick decisions over more strategic ones. Quick, reactive decisions may offer immediate relief but often compound the problem, creating additional layers of complexity, while contributing to long-term decision fatigue. This reactiveness doesn't just impact the individual and productivity—it cascades across teams, potentially affecting the entire organization.

Understanding the deeper impact of decision-making—and the fatigue that follows—is the first step toward reducing its negative consequences. Recognizing how decision fatigue depletes capacity and strategic focus creates an opportunity to approach demands more effectively. By addressing this hidden drain on mental capacity, executives can enhance productivity, creating the conditions for greater clarity, morale, and efficiency across their teams.

Decision-Making in Action

I can say with confidence that it's not common practice to pause and evaluate how we make decisions. Most people simply act, relying on instinct, habit, or past experiences, and then move on without much thought. This approach feels natural, even automatic, leaving little reason to question whether it should be improved. But in today's fast-paced environment, simply acting can come at a cost. Updating decision-making processes is critical for preserving capacity and enhancing productivity. Without deliberate evaluation, inefficiency and larger problems often arise down the road.

For example, imagine you're in a team meeting discussing a project timeline for a new client. With just five minutes left, an email from the client arrives, requesting the deadline be moved up by two weeks. Feeling the pressure to act decisively, you immediately agree, trusting your team will figure out how to make it work. But after the meeting ends and the details sink in, you realize the accelerated timeline will overburden your team, compromise quality, and strain internal relationships. What seemed like a quick, proactive decision now threatens to derail the project and damage team capacity.

This scenario demonstrates how urgency and pressure can lead to reactive decisions, amplifying decision fatigue and creating downstream challenges. As Jeff Bezos, founder of Amazon, the world's largest e-commerce and cloud computing company, wisely noted, "Moving forward quickly on decisions, as quickly as you *responsibly* can, is how you increase velocity."[3] His words highlight the balance leaders must strike: decisiveness paired with responsibility. Rushing a decision may seem effective in the moment, but without careful consideration, it risks compounding fatigue and setbacks.

A structured approach to decision-making could have allowed the executive and team to pause, even briefly, to assess critical variables like capacity demands and potential obstacles. This clarity might have led to negotiating with the client, ensuring a choice that balanced immediate demands with the broader strategic objective.

A Decision-Making Method

I didn't originally set out to create a decision-making method—it emerged naturally over time. My fascination with human behavior—particularly the how and why behind decision-making—led me to reflect on the core elements that influence our decisions. Through my experiences, I noticed that many decisions were loosely grounded in unchecked assumptions. I also observed how the energy executives were willing—or unwilling—to expend played a critical role in shaping their decisions. Similarly, their level of interest often dictated the attention and effort they brought to the process.

As these patterns came into focus—assumptions, energy, and interest—I realized they were the building blocks of decision-making dynamics. Reflecting further, I noticed the first letter of each category aligned perfectly with the vowels AEIOU (and sometimes Y). To complete the method, I identified two final categories—obstacles and (yo)u—rounding out what I now call the AEIOu Method.

A quick side note, the lowercase **u** is not a typo. It's a unique identifier. In the context of the vowel rule, "a-e-i-o-u, and sometimes y", both the **u** and **y** could represent (yo)u, the decision-maker. Since these two letters symbolize the same concept within the developed method, I chose to highlight this unique connection by making the **u** lowercase.

So, what began as a personal observation evolved into a practical and actionable resource. Excited by its potential, I started using the method with clients and quickly recognized its value: it allowed me to ask even more intentional questions, uncover deeper insights, and sometimes preserve capacity for everyone involved.

As my experience with the method grew, I started to wonder if others had a decision-making tool to guide their choices. To my surprise, most didn't; instead, they relied on instinct or habit. Recognizing this gap emphasized the importance of a simple yet effective framework—one designed to enhance clarity and preserve capacity when making decisions.

Understanding the Method

The AEIOu Method provides multiple avenues for making a decision, depending on the complexity and urgency of the situation. It is a flexible thought process tool designed to simplify and offer strength when making decisions. While it may or may not apply to quick, routine decisions, it becomes invaluable when facing significant decisions or delegating tasks to optimize productivity. Taking even five minutes to pause and reflect on the entire method—or only one or two of its categories—can provide the clarity needed to move forward responsibly, sustaining both capacity and progress, while reducing decision fatigue.

Assumptions

Assumptions—whether positive or negative—are often the foundation of decision-making. However, unchecked assumptions can distort perspectives, perpetuate blind spots, and lead to unintended outcomes. By consciously challenging them, you can make decisions that are more accurate and impactful.

Assumptions in Action

An executive decides to offer the team a flexible, hybrid work model, assuming it will boost morale and productivity because it aligns with employee work trends. To make a decision, the executive seeks feedback from the team. It's unanimous, everyone is excited about the idea. Encouraged by this enthusiasm, the executive outlines the vision, confident it will be a win for everyone.

However, within a few months, unforeseen challenges emerge. Communication gaps develop between in-office and remote employees, leading to fragmented conversations and increased friction. Remote team members feel disconnected and often overcompensate by working longer hours, unsure when to start or end their day. Collaborative efforts are no longer deep but instead topical, requiring more meetings to align tasks, further straining productivity and capacity. While the initial assumption was well-intentioned, it failed to account for the complexities of integrating a hybrid model and the support necessary for success.

Leveraging the Method:

Prior to implementing the change, the executive could have leveraged the A in the Method to challenge assumptions by asking:

1. **What assumptions are we making about how hybrid work will influence communication and collaboration?** Answering this could reveal that hybrid work can create gaps in communication between remote and in-office employees. To address this, the executive could introduce tools like real-time messaging platforms or shared project boards, ensuring seamless collaboration. Sticking to regular team-wide check-ins could also help bridge potential communication gaps and align everyone's efforts.

2. **What assumptions are we making about the systems and processes needed to support this shift?** Evaluate whether

existing workflows and tools can effectively support a hybrid structure. For example, the executive might audit current technology to identify gaps and implement updated collaboration tools or provide additional training on existing systems. Additionally, creating clear hybrid work policies, such as expectations for availability and meeting participation, could set the team up for success.

3. **What assumptions are we making about the transition itself?** Transitions often bring unexpected hurdles. To prepare the team, the executive could have organized a pre-launch workshop or series of meetings to discuss potential assumptions. This could have created an opportunity for employees to brainstorm solutions, voice concerns, building a collective sense of readiness for the transition.

By leveraging the A in the Method to evaluate and refine assumptions, the executive and team could have been better prepared for the transition. With this, the hybrid model could have launched with fewer disruptions, preserving productivity and capacity, ensuring both real-time momentum and team morale were maintained.

Key Takeaway:

Assumptions, even those supported by initial enthusiasm, can overlook subtle yet critical factors like real-time collaboration. By using the A in the Method to test and refine assumptions, an executive could avoid common blind spots and foster a more resilient, productive environment. When making decisions, consider: *What am I, or are we, assuming?*

Energy

Energy is a crucial but often underestimated driver of effective decision-making. It shapes how much effort you—or your team—can commit to a decision, influencing both momentum and outcomes. Without assessing energy levels, you risk overloading yourself or others, leading to diminished productivity and unnecessary fatigue.

Energy in Action

An executive plans a major brainstorming session for a new product launch. Enthusiastic about the product, the executive schedules the session for 2:30 p.m. on a Friday, hoping to kick off implementation first thing Monday morning. However, during the meeting, the energy in the room is low. The team seems disengaged, offering fewer ideas than usual, and discussions lack spark. As a result, the session fails to produce collective excitement and determination, leaving the executive frustrated and without the right team excitement. The issue? The meeting's timing didn't account for the team's energy levels after a demanding work week.

Leveraging the Method:

Before scheduling the session, the executive could have leveraged the E in the Method to evaluate energy dynamics by asking:

1. **What energy is realistic to expect from the team during a Friday afternoon session?** Understanding that Friday afternoons are often associated with lower energy, the executive could opt for a shorter session or delay the meeting to a time better aligned with the team's natural energy rhythms.

2. **What energy might pre-meeting preparation spark,**

ensuring everyone is ready to contribute in a meaningful way? By sharing materials and prompts in advance, the executive could help participants arrive with well-formed ideas, reducing the energy drain of generating new concepts on the spot.

By leveraging the E in the Method to assess energy dynamics, the executive could have facilitated a more productive and engaging session, boosting team momentum, fostering a shared sense of enthusiasm.

Key Takeaway:

Energy levels play a critical role in decision-making and execution. Overlooking them can disrupt even the best plans. Aligning decisions with optimal energy levels enhances creativity, focus, and outcomes. Using the E in the Method, you can intentionally assess and prioritize energy to make decisions that maximize capacity. When making decisions, consider: *What energy does this activity require, and how can I, or we, leverage it for the best results?*

Interest

Interest plays a pivotal role in decision-making, directly influencing how much time and effort you or your team are willing to invest in a task. Tasks that spark genuine interest often lead to higher levels of engagement and creativity, while lower interest tasks can feel draining and are more likely to be postponed or avoided. By consciously assessing interest levels—both your own and those of your team—you can allocate resources strategically, ensuring capacity is preserved and outcomes are optimized.

DECISION FATIGUE

Interest in Action

A Vice President of Marketing thrives on creative work, prioritizing tasks like campaign strategy and audience engagement, which she finds exciting and fulfilling. However, her role also requires focusing on less stimulating activities, such as budget reviews and administrative tasks. One day, she receives a meeting request for a team brainstorming session about a new, quick-turnaround campaign, but it conflicts with a previously scheduled budget review meeting.

She knows her participation in both meetings is important, but her schedule is already packed, so she decides to prioritize the budget review, assuming she can catch up on the brainstorming session later. However, during the budget review, she finds her interest fading. Her thoughts repeatedly drift to the brainstorming session, a task she finds far more interesting and aligned with her strengths. When she finally reconnects with the team to review their brainstorming results, she realizes she missed critical momentum. Her delayed involvement left gaps in direction and cost her the opportunity to contribute fresh ideas when they were most needed.

Leveraging the Method:

Before deciding between the two commitments, the executive could have leveraged the I in the Method to evaluate her level of interest and how best to approach both demands by asking:

1. **What interest do I have in contributing directly to each meeting's objectives, and how critical is my involvement?** By assessing her interest and criticality of involvement, the executive might recognize that her strengths and passion would have a greater impact on the brainstorming session, making it the

higher-priority task.

2. What interest does this meeting hold in advancing priorities or the team's goals? Considering the objectives of each meeting, the executive could evaluate how her presence would affect the success of each initiative and adjust accordingly.

3. What interest might a team member have in attending the budget meeting, and how could their involvement support their growth and development? By identifying opportunities to delegate, the budget meeting could have been assumed by a team member who would benefit professionally, ensuring the meeting objectives are met while also supporting the individual's development.

By leveraging the I in the Method, the executive aligns her decisions with her interests and her team's development, preserving capacity, fostering growth, and driving meaningful progress.

Key Takeaway:

Interest plays a critical role in decision-making and execution. By focusing on tasks that align with high-interest activities and thoughtfully addressing low-interest ones, you can optimize your capacity and elevate outcomes. When making decisions, consider: *How does my level of interest in this task, or that of my team, influence my or our approach, and what adjustments can I, or we, make to achieve the best possible results?*

Obstacles

Obstacles are an inevitable part of decision-making. They can derail progress, drain capacity, and create frustration if left unaddressed. While some executives prefer to tackle obstacles as they arise, forecasting them in advance is a far more effective strategy. Anticipating potential obstacles allows you to approach decisions with clarity, build contingency plans, and create a proactive environment where challenges can be lessened before they escalate.

Obstacles in Action

A 10-person tech company decides to roll out a new customer relationship management (CRM) platform to streamline client communication and improve productivity. Without the budget for consulting support, the leadership team selects an "out-of-the-box" solution, believing the transition will be straightforward. Excited by the potential benefits, they fast-track the launch, bypassing key preparation steps like thorough training, data migration planning, and workflow integration to save time and costs.

However, as the rollout begins, significant obstacles emerge. Employees struggle with the new system due to minimal training, leading to delays in adoption and widespread frustration across the team. Data migration issues surface, resulting in missing or misaligned client information that disrupts workflows. Additionally, some staff members resist the change—demonstrating a low capacity for change (a topic we'll explore further in Chapter 5)—and continue relying on outdated, manual processes, bypassing the CRM entirely. This resistance not only hinders adoption but also creates friction within the team. Blinded by the excitement of potential benefits, leadership underestimated the preparation required to ensure a smoother transition.

While the initiative ultimately achieves its goal, the journey takes longer and feels more difficult than anticipated. This highlights how taking time to address critical steps upfront can prevent frustration, maintain morale, and help teams achieve desired outcomes more efficiently.

Leveraging the Method:

Before initiating the rollout, the leadership team could have leveraged the O in the Method to evaluate potential obstacles by asking:

1. **What obstacles might arise with system adoption, and how can we proactively address them to minimize disruption?** The team could identify potential obstacles, such as lack of familiarity with the platform, and plan extra training sessions to build confidence and ease adoption. They could also identify a Change Champion to spearhead training. We'll cover more of this in Chapter 5.

2. **What tools, support, or strategies are needed to accelerate employee buy-in and preparation, fostering a smooth implementation?** By combining pre-launch workshops, accessible user guides, and open forums to address employee concerns, the leadership team could build stronger understanding, mitigating several obstacles. This proactive approach ensures employees feel equipped and engaged, reducing confusion and resistance during implementation.

By leveraging the O in the Method, the leadership team works to identify obstacles in advance, enabling them to implement solutions that streamline the rollout, and minimize disruptions, maintaining team productivity and capacity.

Key Takeaway:

DECISION FATIGUE

Obstacles can feel overwhelming, and the decisions required to anticipate them may initially drain your capacity. However, strategically investing capacity upfront enables you and your team to navigate obstacles more effectively, driving meaningful progress. When making decisions, consider: *What obstacles might I, or we, encounter, and how can I, or we, prepare to overcome them?*

(Yo)u

At the heart of every decision is **you**—your well-being, your mindset, and how each choice impacts your capacity to lead effectively. As a leader, it's easy to overlook your own mental and emotional state when making decisions, especially in high-pressure environments. However, failing to check in with yourself can lead to unnecessary fatigue, diminished clarity, and reactive decision-making that affects both you and your team. Recognizing how decisions align with your capacity, goals, and overall effectiveness is essential for maintaining harmony and sustainable performance.

(Yo)u in Action

A sales director is preparing for a routine, quarterly strategy session with his team. This meeting is pivotal, as the director plans to introduce critical new sales initiatives and set the tone for the next quarter. However, in the days leading up to the meeting, the director has been managing a grueling work schedule filled with back-to-back activities and late-night report reviews. Despite the heavy demands of routine work and preparation, the director proceeds with the meeting.

As the strategy session unfolds, the director's exhaustion becomes increasingly evident to the team. The presentation lacks the clarity and persuasive tone needed to inspire confidence. Sales representatives raise questions that highlight confusion, leading to low enthusiasm for the new initiatives. Instead of leaving the meeting motivated to tackle ambitious sales targets, the team walks away with hesitation and lingering doubts about the proposed direction.

Leveraging the Method:

Before conducting the meeting, the director could have leveraged the u in the Method to assess personal readiness and available capacity by asking:

1. **Am I fully prepared to bring clarity and energy to this session, or do I need to reschedule?** The director might recognize that fatigue is limiting his ability to lead effectively and decides to postpone the meeting by a day, allowing time to recharge.

2. **Are there elements of the session I can delegate or simplify to focus on delivering the most impactful message?** The director could assign team members to handle updates or logistical details, ensuring his capacity is concentrated on delivering the core initiatives and inspiring the team.

3. **I'm exhausted, so what adjustments can I make to ensure my leadership presence energizes the team and builds confidence in the new initiatives?** Recognizing the exhaustion, the director might incorporate interactive elements like a brainstorming exercise or a discussion segment to foster engagement, taking the focus off himself, while inviting the team to contribute energy.

By leveraging the u in the Method, the sales director considers his

DECISION FATIGUE

available capacity, focusing on factors that directly influence his leadership presence and well-being.

Key Takeaway:

The energy and enthusiasm of a leader sets the tone for everything. When your capacity is depleted, it's reflected in how you show up and impacts the team's engagement. Use the u in the Method to prioritize your well-being so you can bring your best to pivotal moments, ensuring momentum and alignment are achieved. When making decisions, consider: *How does my current capacity impact my effectiveness, and what adjustments can I make to show up as my best self?*

Decision-Fatigue and Productivity

The AEIOu Method may feel unfamiliar at first, but as demonstrated through real-world examples, its value is promising. Whether applied as a whole or in parts, it supports stronger decision-making, positioning you and your team to navigate challenges with clarity, confidence, and stability. The return on adopting the Method goes beyond preserving capacity and reducing decision fatigue—it enhances cohesion, boosting productivity. Embracing this approach isn't just about making better decisions; it's a commitment to sustained progress and leadership excellence. The question now is: how will you apply it to shape next steps for you and your team?

"You are one decision away from optimizing individual and team capacity." - Hilani Ellis

Self-Assessment

Answer yes or no to each question.

1. Do you follow a structured process, like the AEIOu Method,

for making decisions?

2. Do you involve your team in the decision-making process to uncover new information and perspectives?

3. Do you consider energy for both yourself and your team when making decisions?

4. Do you consider your level of interest when making decisions?

5. Do you evaluate potential obstacles and anticipate challenges before committing to a decision?

6. Do you adjust your decision-making process when you start to feel mentally drained or overwhelmed?

7. Do you frequently reassess past decisions to learn from them and improve your approach?

Scoring and Guidance

More yes answers: You are proactive and systematic in your approach to decision making. You likely prioritize effectively, adapt well under pressure, and consider energy, obstacles, and collaboration. These habits help you make thoughtful, clear decisions while optimizing capacity and minimizing decision fatigue.

More no answers: Recognizing these patterns is the first step toward advancement. By adopting a structured process, such as the AEIOu Method, you can optimize energy, manage decision fatigue more effectively, and enhance your decision-making process for greater focus and efficiency.

DECISION FATIGUE

Launch Pad

1. **Individual focus:** The next time you're faced with a decision, apply the AEIOu Method to guide your process. Whether you use it in part, or as a whole, it will help you evaluate assumptions, energy, interest, obstacles, and personal impact, leading to a more thoughtful and efficient outcome.

2. **Team collaboration:** In your next team meeting, use the AEIOu Method to facilitate a group discussion. Ask questions like, "What assumptions are we making? How does energy play into this decision? How does interest play a factor? What obstacles might arise? And how will this decision affect everyone's current capacity?"

3. **Accountability with the team:** The next time someone is tasked with presenting a decision, or two, ask them to leverage the AEIOu Method to best articulate their findings. This delegation strategy helps build trust, promotes learning on the job, and increases accountability.

STATUS QUO

"That's not how we do it." "I'm more comfortable with the old process." These phrases are all too common, reflecting a natural preference for what feels familiar—a mindset we often refer to as the status quo. In business, the status quo represents the routines, systems, and habits professionals rely on to create stability and efficiency. These practices, often rooted in past decisions and company traditions, are designed to provide consistency and reduce uncertainty. However, over time, the same structures that once fostered stability can quietly morph into barriers, affecting capacity and innovation. This shift isn't always obvious; the status quo has a way of embedding itself in daily operations, shaping how work gets done without drawing attention to its limitations.

While familiar practices may seem harmless, their impact is both subtle yet significant. Teams may continue meeting deadlines and achieving goals, but these achievements often mask inefficiencies and untapped potential. Leaders may assume, "If it's working, why change it?"—a mindset that leaves little room for questioning whether current practices are quietly holding the organization back. In today's fast-paced business landscape, where adaptability and innovation are critical, this quiet reliance on outdated practices poses a serious risk. The comfort of the status quo can lull organizations into a false sense of security, making it harder to recognize when stagnation has set in.

Faced with this challenge, many companies turn to technological upgrades, believing these investments will disrupt the status quo and drive meaningful progress. These solutions promise efficiency, innovation, and competitive advantage. Yet technology alone is rarely enough. Without rethinking how work gets done, even the most advanced tools can fall short of their potential, leaving organizations frustrated by the disconnect between their aspirations and actual outcomes. True progress demands more than new tools—it requires a deliberate effort to challenge entrenched habits, align workflows with evolving demands, and create a culture ready to embrace change.

Status Quo in the Workplace

Whether you're leading a small business or a large organization, the status quo exists. This reality creates invisible pressure for leaders—a pressure that invites the need to recognize when once-reliable practices have outlived their usefulness. By acknowledging the hidden impact of entrenched routines, executives can uncover opportunities to remodel how work gets done and build the capacity needed to stay competitive in a rapidly evolving landscape.

As Seth Godin, renowned author and entrepreneur, aptly said, "Organizations that destroy the status quo win. Whatever the status quo is, changing it gives you the opportunity to be remarkable."[1] This perspective highlights the transformative power of disrupting the familiar, not for its own sake, but to pave the way for innovation and growth.

Yet, the status quo isn't inherently negative—it often provides stability and efficiency that can be foundational to organizational success. Understanding both its strengths and its limitations is essential. By taking a balanced view of the status quo, executives can better determine when and how to challenge it, ensuring disruption leads to meaningful progress rather than unintended setbacks.

Benefits of Maintaining the Status Quo

Before leaders can effectively remodel outdated practices, it's essential to recognize the strengths that make the status quo appealing and the value it provides in certain contexts. By understanding its benefits, executives can determine when stability serves as a strategic advantage and when it's time to transition. This balanced perspective ensures that transitions build on the strengths of existing systems rather than discarding them outright.

- **Stability** - The status quo offers predictability, which reduces anxiety and fosters a more harmonious work environment. Employees know what to expect, creating a sense of security that enables them to focus on their roles. In industries like healthcare and aviation, stability is critical—consistent routines ensure safety, reliability, and the trust of stakeholders. In such sectors, even small deviations can have significant consequences, making stability an indispensable asset.

- **Efficiency** - Established processes streamline operations by eliminating guesswork and promoting consistency. When roles, responsibilities, and workflows are clearly defined, tasks are completed more efficiently. For example, manufacturing industries rely on standardized procedures to minimize errors and maximize output. These processes allow teams to execute their tasks with precision, ensuring consistency across operations, boosting overall productivity.

- **Reliability** - The status quo often serves as a safeguard against uncertainty, ensuring that core operations remain consistent and predictable. This reliability is especially valuable in environments where disruptions can have significant consequences. For example, legacy financial institutions rely on established systems to protect their reputation, maintain trust, and comply with stringent regulatory requirements. By prioritizing reliability, these organizations minimize operational risks, maintain customer confidence, and ensure continuity in a highly regulated environment.

Recognizing the strengths of the status quo is important, but it's equally critical to understand where it falls short, especially in environments that demand adaptability and innovation.

Limitations of Maintaining the Status Quo

While the benefits of the status quo provide stability and predictability, they can also create blind spots and hinder capacity. What feels reliable can slowly become restrictive, holding teams back from responding to disruption, capitalizing on opportunities. Recognizing these limitations is essential for executives who aim to create harmony from the strengths of established systems with the agility needed for advancement.

- **Complacency** - One of the most significant dangers of the

CAPACITY: THE NEW ADVANTAGE

status quo is complacency. When organizations become too comfortable with existing conditions, they may stop seeking improvement or innovation. This not only impacts productivity and capacity but also invites stagnation and a loss of competitive advantage. Imagine if Apple stopped delivering new phone models, content to rest on the success of its early designs. Without consistent innovation, even the most successful companies risk being left behind.

- **Resistance to Change** - The more deeply entrenched the status quo, the harder it becomes to implement change. Employees and leaders alike may resist new ideas or approaches, fearing the unknown or clinging to the comfort of familiarity. This resistance often hinders process improvement efforts, reducing productivity and capacity. Consider SpaceX's breakthrough with Falcon 9—a partially reusable rocket that revolutionized the aerospace industry by significantly lowering costs.[2] Had the company followed traditional, disposable rocket practices it would have missed an opportunity to disrupt the market and expand its capacity for future missions.

- **Missed Opportunities** - In today's rapidly evolving business landscape, sticking to the status quo can mean missing critical opportunities. Organizations that fail to adapt to new technologies, market trends, or customer desires risk falling behind more innovative competitors. For example, Netflix's decision to pivot from DVD rentals to streaming video disrupted an entire industry, while competitors who clung to their old models struggled to stay relevant.[3] A reluctance to evolve can drain team capacity, stifle creativity, and prevent companies from reaching their full potential.

While the status quo offers short-term familiarity and efficiency, today's executives must discern when these established practices are no longer serving the organization. Harmonizing between the stability of the known with the potential of the new is key to maximizing capacity and fostering growth. Those who can challenge the status quo—without losing the strengths it offers—position themselves and their organizations to drive innovation, discover more capacity, and secure long-term success.

The Executive's Role in Challenging the Status Quo

For many executives, the responsibilities of leadership already feel monumental. Balancing strategic goals, team development, and operational demands leaves little room to consider taking on what might seem like an added challenge. Yet, addressing the status quo isn't about adding more to your already full platter—it's about ensuring what's already there serves the organization's evolving needs. While it may seem daunting, challenging the status quo offers transformative advantages, revealing pathways for innovation, growth, and capacity expansion.

Executives who approach the status quo with intentionality and curiosity can uncover inefficiencies and turn them into opportunities. The process doesn't mean discarding what works; it means thoughtfully remodeling practices to better align with current demands and future goals. By recognizing the positive impact of disrupting outdated norms, executives can create environments where teams thrive and organizations stay competitive.

Two traits are particularly vital when looking to challenge the status quo: 1) adaptability, which enables executives to navigate uncertainty with agility, and 2) courage, which fuels bold decisions that push beyond the familiar and toward innovation.

- **Adaptability** - Breaking away from the status quo requires more than strategic planning—it demands adaptability. In a rapidly evolving business landscape, the ability to pivot is critical. Adaptive executives cultivate a culture that embraces disruption, encouraging teams to explore new approaches and experiment with innovative ideas. This openness not only drives productivity but also positions organizations to respond effectively to emerging challenges and opportunities.

For example, when Satya Nadella became CEO of Microsoft, the company was struggling to keep pace with competitors. Instead of clinging to legacy strategies, Nadella promoted a culture of adaptability. Under his leadership, teams began developing new capabilities alongside their work on cloud technology and artificial intelligence. This shift challenged Microsoft's status quo, creating new capacity for growth and innovation. Nadella once shared in a McKinsey interview, "At some point, the concept or the idea that made you successful is going to run out of gas."[4] His approach wasn't about predicting every trend—it was about building a responsive, adaptable organization capable of thriving amid disruption and uncertainty.

- **Courage** - While adaptability allows organizations to respond to disruption, courage drives leaders to initiate it. Challenging the status quo requires executives to confront uncertainty, make bold decisions, and lead their teams through the discomfort of disruption. True progress often involves weighing risks and rewards (a concept we'll explore further in the next chapter), accepting potential setbacks, and maintaining focus on long-term goals.

Mary Barra, CEO of General Motors, exemplifies this kind of courageous leadership. When she assumed her role in 2014, GM was grappling with a recall crisis and intense competition in the race for electric and autonomous vehicle production. Barra's willingness to challenge entrenched practices and embrace innovative approaches helped GM strengthen its position in the competitive automotive technology market. "As a leader, I instill the importance of always acting with integrity," Barra once shared. "To me, this means being driven by ingenuity and innovation, having the courage to do and say what's difficult, and taking accountability for results."[5] Her bold decisions disrupted GM's status quo and played a pivotal role in the company's resurgence.

These examples illustrate how adaptability and courage can reshape an organization's trajectory. Recognizing the need for change is a pivotal first step. From there, the executive can take deliberate steps to remodel the status quo and uncover new opportunities for innovation and progress.

Remodeling the Status Quo

Imagine an organization where teams feel energized by their work, finding purpose in progress rather than merely checking boxes. Remodeling the status quo offers this possibility—not as a burden, but as an opportunity to spark excitement about more effective and rewarding ways of working. While the idea of remodeling the status quo might initially seem overwhelming, it doesn't have to be. The path forward often begins with small, deliberate steps that reduce inefficiencies and open the door to lasting advantages.

Consider the example of a team bogged down by lengthy,

unproductive meetings. Instead of a sweeping overhaul, an executive might introduce a simple change: implementing a rule that all meetings must include a clear agenda and honor a max time limit of 30 minutes. This small adjustment can drastically improve focus and productivity, freeing up capacity for more meaningful work. Over time, such shifts not only address inefficiencies but also inspire confidence in the value of adopting new practices.

This process isn't about throwing away what works but remodeling it to meet evolving demands. When leaders guide their teams toward meaningful remodeling, they build capacity, foster innovation, and reinvigorate a shared sense of purpose. Small wins and deliberate action build the confidence and momentum needed to pursue larger breakthroughs.

However, remodeling is rarely straightforward. While some may feel energized by the spark of a new way of working, others may hold tightly to familiar routines, held back by fear or uncertainty. To sustain progress and move forward together, leaders must address this hesitation with intention, ensuring that no one is left behind.

Overcoming Resistance

Resistance is a natural reaction to disruption, rooted in the comfort of what feels safe and familiar. For leaders aiming to remodel the status quo, navigating resistance isn't just a challenge—it's an opportunity. Peter Drucker, often regarded as the father of modern management, famously said, "If you want something new, you have to stop doing something old."[6] His insight highlights the need for disruption. It may unsettle routines, but disruption is the catalyst for innovation and growth.

Research from McKinsey & Company reveals that around 70 percent of disruption initiatives fail, primarily due to resistance and inadequate management support.[7] These failures underscore the vital role executives play in addressing concerns, creating a foundation for successful disruption. To transform resistance into an asset, executives can foster a culture that doesn't just tolerate innovation but actively embraces it.

Key Strategies for Overcoming Resistance:

1. **Plan with Clarity** - Clearly articulate the benefits of the disruption and connect it to the organization's broader goals. Uncertainty thrives in ambiguity; providing a clear vision minimizes fear and builds confidence.

2. **Involve Stakeholders Early** - Engage key individuals and teams from the outset. Their involvement generates buy-in and ensures the disruption feels collaborative rather than imposed.

3. **Foster Transparency** - Ongoing communication builds trust. Teams are more likely to embrace disruption when they understand why it's happening, how it will impact them, and what the intended outcomes are.

Michael Karnjanaprakorn, former CEO of Skillshare—an online learning community, emphasized the importance of communication: "The biggest lesson I've learned as CEO is the art of overcommunicating. I'm constantly repeating the vision of the company to our team. When I thought I couldn't overcommunicate anymore, I would reiterate the vision again."[8] This relentless focus on transparency and repetition ensures that the enthusiasm for disruption permeates the organization, minimizing resistance, fostering excitement.

While resistance is inevitable, it doesn't have to derail progress. Executives who address concerns early, foster collaboration, and maintain open communication can transform resistance into momentum.

Maintaining Momentum

Disruption can be turned into an opportunity for growth when handled with intention. Executives who address concerns early and foster collaboration, create a foundation where momentum builds naturally. Remodeling outdated practices isn't an overnight transformation; instead, it's a journey of incremental progress, where small, deliberate steps pave the way for lasting impact.

Meaningful disruption is the engine behind sustained momentum. It ensures that efforts to challenge the status quo result in capacity expansion and tangible improvements over time. By encouraging experimentation, celebrating wins—no matter how small—and aligning efforts with long-term goals, executives can turn disruption into a shared endeavor. This approach not only keeps teams engaged but also reinforces the idea that progress is a journey, not a destination.

Practical Steps for Creating Momentum:

Here are three actionable ways to build momentum as you disrupt the status quo in your organization:

1. **Conduct a Status Quo Audit** - Evaluate current processes, tools, and routines to identify areas that no longer align with your organization's goals. Collaborate with your team by asking targeted questions: What's one process that feels outdated or inefficient? Where do we encounter the most delays or frustrations? This exercise not only uncovers

opportunities for improvement but also fosters employee buy-in by involving them in the process.

2. **Pilot a Small Disruption Plan** - Start with a manageable initiative that targets a specific inefficiency. For example, test a new collaboration tool within one department or adjust the format of a recurring meeting for three weeks. Use feedback and outcomes to refine your approach before scaling the remodeling across the organization. This measured approach reduces unnecessary disruption while providing clear evidence of how intentional shifts can improve both efficiency and outcomes.

3. **Celebrate and Share Early Wins** - Recognize and highlight even the smallest successes to build excitement and engagement. For example, if a streamlined process saves time or reduces errors, acknowledge the achievement in a team meeting or a quick email. Sharing these wins reinforces the value of remodeling and keeps the team motivated to continue the journey.

Disrupting the status quo isn't about upending everything at once—it's about incrementally remodeling how your organization thinks, collaborates, and grows. Leaders who prioritize adaptability, courage, and incremental progress inspire their teams to move beyond the familiar, resulting in expanded capacity.

As you reflect on your organization's status quo, remember this: disruption doesn't have to be chaotic. It can be deliberate, measured, and deeply rewarding. Start with a single step, build momentum, and watch as your team rises to meet a future filled with untapped potential and expanded capacity.

CAPACITY: THE NEW ADVANTAGE

"Maintaining the status quo inevitably leads to falling behind."
- Hilani Ellis

Self-Assessment

Answer yes or no to each question.

1. Do you actively identify areas where existing processes or practices may no longer align with current goals?
2. Does your team feel supported in proposing and testing new ideas without fear of failure?
3. Do you prioritize addressing inefficiencies that impact capacity or hinder progress?
4. Do you encourage cross-departmental collaboration to uncover and address outdated practices?
5. Do you encourage your team to reflect on and share feedback about how current practices might be improved?
6. Are team members regularly involved in discussions about how to improve workflows and achieve better results?
7. Do you foster a culture where small, incremental improvements are valued as much as larger changes?

Scoring and Guidance

More yes answers: You're creating an environment where disruption is managed thoughtfully, encouraging your team to challenge the status quo in ways that expand capacity and drive progress. Keep building on these strengths by maintaining open communication and refining processes regularly.

More no answers: You may be leaning too heavily on traditional approaches, which could stifle innovation and limit capacity. Start by addressing one or two areas where incremental change could have the most significant impact, fostering a mindset of adaptability and continuous improvement.

Launch Pad

1. **Encourage innovation:** Foster an environment where team members feel encouraged to share their ideas, no matter how small. Set up a dedicated email address like *ideas@companyemail.com* for submissions and form a small team or committee to review ideas monthly. Recognize and reward contributions to keep momentum going—this shows that even small innovations can have a big impact.

2. **Foster collaboration:** Break down silos between departments by encouraging cross-functional collaboration. Consider implementing a job-shadowing program where employees spend half a day learning about roles in other departments. This exposure helps teams rethink established workflows and challenge conventional approaches. By sharing diverse perspectives, teams can disrupt the status quo and find new ways to increase capacity and drive innovation across the organization.

3. **Embrace continuous improvement:** Make it a habit to regularly (this could be quarterly) review and update processes. Instead of relying on "the way things have always been done," check in with your team to uncover where processes might be slowing them down. Understanding your team's capacity for change (a concept we'll explore in more detail in Chapter 5) and ensuring incremental adjustments will lead to sustainable improvements.

RISK REWARD

In the business world, risk is often viewed through the lens of risk management—the practice of identifying, assessing, and mitigating threats to minimize disruptions and avoid costly errors. For many executives, this approach feels instinctive, a safeguard designed to shield their organization and people from negative outcomes. It's a mindset that prioritizes steadiness, offering a sense of control in an ever-evolving business landscape.

But what if risk isn't just something to mitigate but a catalyst to opportunity? While risk management emphasizes avoiding pitfalls, it often overlooks its essential counterpart: **reward**. Every risk carries the possibility of a gain, and focusing solely on minimizing threats may unintentionally close the door on growth, innovation, and capacity expansion.

Adopting a risk-reward mindset broadens how executives evaluate opportunities. Instead of only asking, "What could go wrong?" they might also ask, "What could go right?" This shift transforms risk from a defensive exercise into a strategic tool for exploration and growth. By evaluating risks alongside rewards, executives can direct resources to initiatives with the greatest potential impact, fostering bold innovation and encouraging teams to explore new possibilities without fear of failure.

Consider an organization entering a high-potential yet uncertain market. Focusing solely on risks without integrating the potential for reward limits access to the full picture. Challenges like competition, regulatory hurdles, and market volatility are valid concerns, but when paired with potential rewards—such as reaching untapped customers, achieving revenue growth, or securing a competitive advantage—they create a more complete evaluation. By evaluating these factors together, executives can reframe uncertainty as an opportunity. This unified approach ensures that actions are both strategic and sustainable, paving the way for impactful progress while minimizing costly missteps.

However, a risk-reward mindset alone isn't enough. Its success depends on understanding and aligning with the **risk capacity** of the individuals and teams tasked with execution. Understanding the risk capacity of team members, helps executives navigate uncertainty more effectively, fostering sustainable progress and ensuring strategies are actionable and enduring.

Understanding Risk Capacity

Risk capacity defines how individuals navigate uncertainty and how they approach both challenges and opportunities. It's not a one-size-fits-all state but rather one that exists on a spectrum. On one end, those with low-risk capacity prioritize stability, focusing on mitigating risks to maintain consistency. On the other end, individuals with high-risk capacity embrace uncertainty, viewing risks as opportunities for growth and innovation.

However, many individuals can fall somewhere in the middle of this spectrum, with their approach often influenced by circumstances. They might lean toward caution in high-risk scenarios but adopt a more flexible mindset when the potential rewards align with individual or team strengths or overall goals.

It's also important to note that bias plays a significant role in shaping how risks are perceived and acted upon. Cognitive biases, such as overconfidence, can distort judgment, influencing decisions and outcomes. We'll explore the impact of bias and how it intersects with risk capacity later in this chapter.

For organizations, leveraging risk capacity at all levels is essential for aligning team strengths with the demands of the business. A team member who thrives on stability can provide a grounding perspective during high-risk scenarios, while those more inclined to embrace uncertainty may drive exploratory or growth-focused initiatives. Discovering and utilizing these differences enables executives to position individuals where they can have the greatest impact.

This approach fosters a flexible and collaborative environment, ensuring challenges are addressed strategically and opportunities are maximized. By aligning individual strengths with organizational objectives, executives pave the way for steady and sustainable risk taking.

Discovering Individual Risk Capacity

Discovering an individual's risk capacity may initially seem like an added responsibility, but the insights it provides are invaluable. These insights help executives position team members for success, ensuring that risks are approached with strategic clarity. With this understanding, risk taking becomes an opportunity for growth, and risk-reward pursuits are undertaken with confidence, paving the way for both individual and team achievement.

Consider a mid-sized company navigating a complex market expansion. As the leadership team discusses their strategy, the CEO takes note of how each team member responds to the plan and risks involved. One, known for thriving in new situations, proposed innovative solutions to capture untapped market share. Another, detail-oriented and methodical, anticipated potential regulatory challenges and suggested strategies to mitigate them. By aligning each person's strengths with the demands of the project, the CEO struck harmony between bold exploration and meticulous execution. This synergy not only resulted in a timely market entry but also fostered a dynamic within the team where differing approaches were seen as complementary rather than conflicting.

As illustrated in the above scenario, effectively identifying each team member's risk capacity starts with observation rather than assumption. Executives often default to believing their teams share a similar risk threshold, but in reality, individuals respond to uncertainty differently. By paying close attention to responses, executives can recognize strengths and align contributions with organizational goals, creating an environment where diverse approaches to risk are valued. The strategies below offer practical ways to assess and adapt to varying risk capacities, ensuring that each team member is positioned to contribute at their fullest potential.

- **Observe patterns under pressure** - Notice how team members handle ambiguity. Those with high-risk capacity often embrace newness and propose bold solutions, while others gravitate toward measured, predictable approaches. Both perspectives are valuable when balanced effectively.

- **Engage in one-on-one discussions** - Conversations about past experiences with new or risky situations can reveal how team members approached uncertainty and what support they needed. These insights help executives align future tasks with individual strengths, enhancing team effectiveness and progress.

- **Facilitate simulated scenarios** - Controlled challenges or role-playing exercises illuminate how team members perceive and approach risks, especially in unfamiliar or unpredictable contexts. These simulations often uncover hidden assumptions, such as overestimating potential rewards or underestimating obstacles. Recognizing these perspectives fosters thoughtful planning and preparation for future risk endeavors.

When executives leverage the above strategies, they cultivate an environment where each team member's unique approach to risk not only strengthens collaboration but also inspires confidence in navigating uncertainty. This focus on risk capacity helps align individual strengths with collective goals, creating the foundation for meaningful growth and progress.

To see the transformative potential of high-risk capacity in action, consider the story of Sara Blakely, founder of Spanx, a shapewear brand. Her journey illustrates how one end of the risk capacity spectrum can turn risk-taking into remarkable success.

A Real-Life Example of High-Risk Capacity

Each week, Sara Blakely's father would ask her, "What did you fail at this week?"[1] By reframing failure as a stepping stone for growth, he encouraged her to see risk as an opportunity rather than something to avoid. Shaped by this unconventional approach,

Blakely's ability to embrace risk was cultivated early.

With no prior experience in fashion or launching a business, Blakely's willingness to take a risk drove her to invest her $5,000 life savings into her vision. She faced numerous obstacles, from struggling to secure hosiery manufacturers to overcoming skepticism from industry insiders. Despite the countless setbacks, each challenge was met with strategic thinking and resilience, enabling her to transform Spanx into a billion-dollar brand that redefined an industry and set a new standard. [2]

Blakely's journey highlights how her overconfidence bias, a common trap in which strong belief distorts perception, contributed to the way she evaluated risk. While she faced repeated skepticism and rejection from industry experts, she remained convinced there was real consumer demand for her product. By constantly reflecting on her strategy, Blakely balanced passion with strategic evaluation, ensuring her risks were intentional, therefore offering a path to sustainable reward. Her story is a testament to the power of self-awareness—showing that true success stems not just from belief in the vision, but from the discipline to evaluate and evolve the strategy driving it.

How Bias Impacts Risk Capacity

The way executives perceive risk isn't always as objective as they think. Biases—mental shortcuts in thinking—can shape how executives perceive risks, rewards, and their capacity to act. For instance, overconfidence bias might cause an executive to over believe in their vision or underestimate obstacles, creating blind spots that influence their strategy.

To fully harness risk capacity and maximize risk-reward

opportunities, it's important for executives to recognize how biases can distort their perception of the unknown. Overconfidence, anchoring, confirmation, and expertise biases each affect how risks are perceived, often influencing strategic endeavors. By identifying and addressing these tendencies, executives can strengthen risk capacity, equipping themselves and their teams to pursue opportunities with greater clarity, balance, and consistency.

Navigating Bias to Cultivate Risk Capacity

Overconfidence Bias

Overestimating one's knowledge or abilities.

> **Example:** Sara Blakely's confidence in her vision drove her to persevere through challenges, but it also led her to initially underestimate obstacles, such as finding a willing manufacturer. However, her perseverance and adaptability helped her balance this bias, ensuring her optimism was grounded in reality.
>
> **Solution:** Seek external feedback and conduct thorough assessments to align decisions with realistic risks and potential rewards. This ensures confidence translates into actionable, balanced efforts.

Anchoring Bias

Relying too heavily on initial information, even when new evidence emerges.

> **Example:** An executive sets aggressive sales targets based on past success but hesitates to adjust when market research reveals declining demand. This rigidity strains resources and misses opportunities to pivot toward attainable goals.

Solution: Encourage adaptability as a strength in managing risk and reward. Reassess information regularly and weigh updated data to balance risks and rewards effectively.

Confirmation Bias
Favoring information that supports preexisting beliefs while dismissing contrary evidence.

Example: An executive backs a high-risk product launch based on internal enthusiasm while ignoring external market signals of customer hesitancy. This selective focus leads to overinvestment and missed opportunities elsewhere.

Solution: Explore diverse perspectives and critical feedback during the planning phase. Implement structured evaluation strategies to examine both supporting and opposing evidence for balanced, informed planning.

Expertise Bias
Over relying on personal expertise, leading to unrealistic expectations.

Example: A CEO expects a new employee to quickly match their pace and fully grasp company processes within 30 days, leading to unrealistic pressure and misaligned expectations.

Solution: Cultivate an onboarding process that emphasizes steady growth, offering time and capacity for knowledge-building. This approach reduces unnecessary pressure, aligns expectations and fosters sustainable, high-performing talent.

In my experience, expertise bias has shown up in nearly eighty-five percent of the leaders I've had the opportunity to work alongside. One client, a founder and CEO of a national hospitality brand, illustrated this trait firsthand. Thirty days after placing a new executive team member, I checked in to see how things were progressing. His response reflected a common struggle for people with expertise bias: "Hilani, I would have expected Jennifer to be more up to speed by now, offering suggestions to optimize how we work." His frustration wasn't about performance alone—it was a classic case of expertise bias shaping unrealistic expectations of Jennifer's risk capacity at this stage.

With over 30 years of experience founding and scaling his company, the CEO had developed an intuitive, fast-paced work style, where navigating uncertainty had become second nature. His comfort with risk-taking was the result of years spent making high-stakes decisions in an environment he knew inside and out. But Jennifer, new to her role and the company, was still acclimating—her risk capacity was naturally lower as she worked to understand the company's culture, processes, and unspoken expectations. Hesitant to make bold suggestions too soon, she was in the necessary phase of gathering knowledge before stepping into greater risk-taking.

I explained that Jennifer's initial hesitation wasn't a limitation but a normal stage of building risk capacity—developing the confidence and knowledge to make high-impact decisions. By realigning expectations and allowing space for growth, the CEO not only set Jennifer up for greater success but also strengthened their collaboration. This shift created the conditions for Jennifer to expand her capacity, contribute strategically, and ultimately take on risk with greater precision, aligning her efforts with the executive's and company's long-term goals.

Leadership and the Evolution of Risk Capacity

Leadership is not just about making decisions or setting strategies—it's about cultivating an environment where individuals and teams can thrive, even in the face of uncertainty. Risk capacity plays a pivotal role in this process. Throughout this chapter, we've explored how understanding and leveraging risk capacity can help leaders drive progress, foster innovation, and create harmony within their organizations (we'll talk more about harmony inside organizations in Chapter 7). As a leader, your role is to recognize and nurture this capacity—not only in yourself but also in those you lead.

The story of Sara Blakely demonstrated how high-risk capacity, when paired with thoughtful reflection, can transform passion into remarkable success. On the other hand, Jennifer's journey highlighted the importance of patience and alignment when developing risk capacity. These examples remind us that risk capacity exists on a spectrum, evolving with experience, confidence, and trust. Leaders who understand this evolution are better positioned to guide their teams toward meaningful and sustainable risk-taking.

Biases, as we've discussed, add complexity to understanding and leveraging risk capacity. They shape how risks are perceived and acted upon, often creating blind spots that could hinder progress and outcomes. But when leaders work intentionally to discover and address these biases—whether it's overconfidence or expertise—they refine their perception, providing clarity for their teams. This clarity lays the groundwork for steady pursuits to risk-reward endeavors, enabling resilience and innovation to flourish.

By focusing on growing risk capacity—both within yourself and your teams—leaders create environments where challenges become risk-reward opportunities. It's not about eliminating uncertainty but about approaching it with the confidence and tools needed to drive progress. The clarity gained from understanding these dynamics enables leaders to act decisively, foster collaboration, positioning their teams for success. How will you use these insights to shape a future of meaningful risk-taking?

"The greatest achievements often lie just beyond the edge of our comfort zones, where risk meets reward." - Hilani Ellis

Self-Assessment

Answer yes or no to each question.

1. Do you consistently evaluate both potential risks and rewards before committing to significant decisions?

2. Have you implemented a clear process to identify, assess, and balance risk-reward dynamics across your organization?

3. Do you actively pursue growth opportunities that involve calculated risks, fostering both innovation and resilience?

4. Before assigning high-stakes projects, do you assess both your team's risk capacity and the resources required to sustain progress?

5. Do you create opportunities for open dialogue about risks, rewards, and potential biases to promote thoughtful decision-making?

6. Does your organization regularly reflect on risk-reward outcomes to enhance future decision-making and collaboration?

7. Do you encourage team members to contribute their perspectives when evaluating potential risks and rewards?

Scoring and Guidance

More yes answers: You demonstrate strong leadership when it comes to navigating risk-reward dynamics. You're fostering a culture of thoughtful risk-taking balancing innovation with caution. This strengthens adaptability, promotes collaboration, and ensures your organization remains open to taking risks.

More no answers: There may be opportunities to refine how you assess and manage risk within your team or organization. Strengthening your process for evaluating risks, fostering open dialogue, and encouraging strategic reflection can enhance decision-making and confidence. With small, intentional adjustments, you can cultivate a culture that embraces calculated risks—leading to more informed decisions, sustainable growth, and long-term success.

Launch Pad

1. **Observe, don't overanalyze:** Pay attention to how team members handle ambiguity in everyday situations. Do they lean toward bold solutions, or do they prefer measured, predictable approaches? This simple observation helps you better understand their risk capacity without requiring formal assessments or additional tasks. The intention is not to change the behavior but to understand the role they can play in future opportunities.

2. **The bias check:** In your next team discussion or planning meeting, ask: "What are we assuming to be true about this situation, and how could we test or validate it?" This question

directly addresses potential biases in a non-confrontational way by inviting the team to explore their thought process together. It encourages actionable reflection and opens the door to uncovering blind spots while keeping the conversation constructive.

3. **The essential project question:** When embarking on a risky project, include this question in your planning process: "How will this decision impact both our short-term and long-term capacity?" This ensures that you're considering not just the immediate risks and rewards but also the resources, energy, and focus required to sustain progress.

CHANGE CAPACITY

Ever wondered why some team members thrive in times of change while others seem to hesitate? In the ever-evolving business world, the ability to adapt to change isn't merely a desirable work quality—it's essential. While change management focuses on structured processes to navigate specific transitions, change capacity offers something more meaningful. It shifts the focus from systems to people, revealing the interests, adaptability, and capacity within individuals and teams to embrace change. Whether it's adopting new technologies, responding to shifting market demands, or remodeling workflows, navigating change remains a constant for modern teams. By helping executives understand not just how people respond to change but why, change capacity becomes a powerful tool for driving productivity and progress.

This need to understand change at a deeper level is underscored by an Orgvue survey of 700 executives, in which 38% admitted they'd rather quit their job than manage another change initiative.[1] This finding clearly signals that executives are feeling the strain of constant change—and if they are, it's likely their teams are too. Change fatigue is real, and its impact can derail even the most well-intentioned initiatives. By exploring change capacity, executives can uncover practical ways to address this fatigue, building resilience across their organization.

The first step in understanding change capacity is to move beyond the assumption that teams have limitless capacity for change. It's about recognizing individual strengths, uncovering opportunities, and addressing challenges in a way that aligns efforts with evolving demands. Executives who do this not only enhance their team's adaptability but also lay the foundation for meaningful and sustainable momentum.

Understanding Individual Change Capacity

Like risk capacity, change capacity is not fixed. While there are generally two primary levels of change capacity—low and high—these levels are dynamic and context-dependent. A team member's capacity for change can vary based on factors like workload, personal circumstances or interest. Interest, in particular, plays a crucial role in how someone engages with change. When the change aligns with career aspirations, a team member's willingness to embrace it increases. Conversely, when there's a disconnect with the proposed change, resistance can naturally follow.

Rather than viewing change capacity on a scale of better or worse, it's important to recognize the complementary strengths that both low and high change capacity bring. Low change capacity can provide stability, consistency, and a thoughtful approach to evaluating change, ensuring details aren't overlooked. On the other hand, high change capacity fuels exploration and innovation, moving initiatives forward with curiosity and energy. Leaders who account for the different change capacity levels within their teams, can develop a more nuanced approach—one that not only positions the right people for the right changes but also fosters collaboration, alignment, and a smoother transition for the entire team.

Discovering Low Change Capacity

Understanding low change capacity within your team isn't just about addressing hesitations—it's about creating pathways for progress. Recognizing where team members may struggle with change equips executives to provide targeted guidance and foster adaptability. By addressing these areas thoughtfully, executives can encourage and support individuals to step beyond their comfort zones, strengthening the team's overall capacity for collaboration and progress. Team members with lower change capacity often gravitate toward stability, relying on familiar methods to maintain consistency. They may hesitate to embrace new initiatives, show resistance, or prefer sticking to established routines—even when small adjustments are introduced. This tendency can result in slower engagement with innovative projects or delay timelines, as these individuals need more time to adjust.

When I think about low change capacity, I think about my work with a CFO of a global company—we'll call him Frank. This was my second time working with the company, but since Frank had only joined the company five weeks prior, it was our first time collaborating. When engaging with new executives, I use our initial meeting to establish trust and build rapport. After building a connection with Frank, I introduced him to the specialized and proprietary candidate vetting process I designed in 2017, which goes beyond traditional resume filtering to assess a candidate's full potential.

CAPACITY: THE NEW ADVANTAGE

As I began to share my screen, to walk Frank through a sample candidate portfolio, he interrupted saying, "This isn't how I usually like to work. I typically just look over a resume, compile questions, then decide who to meet."

Frank's response surprised me. In my eight years of talent acquisition work, clients typically find the depth of the vetting process compelling, as it saves valuable time and capacity by presenting only top-tier candidates in a third-round vetting stage. However, I quickly realized that Frank was still adjusting to a new role and organization. His preference for simplicity and familiar processes suggested that my comprehensive approach might be testing his change capacity limits. Likely juggling a flood of newness and competing priorities, he may have seen my vetting process as just one more unfamiliar layer to comprehend and manage.

The search launched, and I adhered to my process knowing the insights it yields are instrumental in identifying stronger candidates. After several weeks in the market, I submitted candidate portfolios, even though I anticipated he might only focus on the resumes, and we connected over a briefing call. I opened with a question, "What excites you about candidate X?" Frank responded by only focusing on potential red flags, rather than any positives. This response was telling.

Rather than focusing on the possibilities, Frank's priority was to zero in on potential risks, a common strategy among low change capacity individuals, as a way to maintain understanding and stability. While a cautious approach can serve a purpose, it can also lead to missed opportunities when over-relied upon. That's why understanding change capacity is valuable—it helps executives recognize when hesitation serves a purpose and when it unnecessarily limits progress and potential.

Traits of Individuals with Low Change Capacity:

- **Stability** - They often gravitate toward established routines and prefer sticking with familiar methods.

- **Risk-awareness** - They are cautious when new projects or workflows are presented, often taking extra time to evaluate potential impacts.

- **Thoughtful approach** - They may approach conversations about change with caution, needing additional information or reassurance before fully engaging.

Strategies for Maximizing Low Change Capacity:

- **Be clear about the change** - Lean into their preference for detailed information by clearly outlining the scope, purpose, and expected outcomes of upcoming changes. This supports their need for clarity and helps prevent avoidable resistance.

- **Involve them in change planning** - Invite them to contribute to the change rollout, particularly in designing phased approaches.

- **Audit change concerns** - Use the AEIOu Method to uncover deeper concerns they may have about the change. This structured process can also surface blind spots the broader team may have missed.

By recognizing and working with these traits, you can help team members gradually build their confidence in navigating change, fostering a more cohesive and supportive work environment. Their cautious, measured approach offers distinct value, ensuring changes are thoughtfully vetted and risks are fully considered.

When paired with the curiosity and agility of high change capacity team members, both styles complement each other—grounding progress in both stability and momentum, ultimately strengthening the team's ability to drive sustainable productivity and growth.

Discovering High Change Capacity

High change capacity team members bring a readiness for the unknown that fuels exploration and progress. They don't just adapt to change—they lean into it, seeing new challenges as opportunities. Their readiness to engage thoughtfully in discussions about change and explore innovative solutions makes them key drivers of meaningful evolution.

Beyond their ability to navigate uncertainty, they bring an adaptable energy that can inspire those around them. They actively engage in it, leading exploration efforts, guiding peers who may find change more challenging. Their adaptability and flexibility create momentum in dynamic environments, ensuring progress isn't just possible—but sustainable.

When I think of high change capacity, I'm reminded of a time when I worked with a global investment firm in the travel and leisure industry—a company valued at several billion dollars—where a team's high change capacity brought enthusiasm and engaging energy to the hiring process. In a meeting with one of the managing partners and his team of seven, I introduced my approach to finding top talent; the team was instantly receptive. As I explained how the approach would streamline our efforts, their curiosity was palpable. They eagerly asked questions, intrigued by how this deeply vetted process could make the hiring objective more effective and enjoyable.

CHANGE CAPACITY

For this team, embracing change wasn't a leap; it was a logical step toward greater productivity and effectiveness. Their approach highlights the advantage of high change capacity—an openness to new ideas that not only enhances efficiency but also frees up resources, saving much needed capacity.

Traits of Individuals with High Change Capacity:

- **Comfort with ambiguity** - Open to exploring new paths even when all the answers aren't clear yet, trusting that progress can happen without perfect certainty.

- **Opportunity-focused mindset** - Naturally sees shifts and challenges as openings for progress, rather than barriers.

- **Intentional pacing** - Understands that progress during change is rarely linear, so they balance urgency with reflection, making room for adjustment as needed.

Strategies for Maximizing High Change Capacity:

- **Leverage their curiosity** - Provide opportunities to explore emerging trends, pilot new processes, or evaluate innovations that could benefit the organization. Their natural desire to seek what's next can uncover valuable opportunities before they're obvious to everyone else.

- **Position as change champions** - Provide opportunities to lead change initiatives or influence others who may be hesitant. These team members can help build trust and momentum for change (more on this in a moment).

- **Create collaborative opportunities** - Involve them in cross-functional projects or brainstorming sessions. Their adaptive mindset and creativity could drive innovative solutions across departments.

Understanding the traits and potential of high change capacity individuals is only part of the equation. To fully harness their impact, executives must intentionally identify and position these team members where their openness, curiosity, and influence can drive meaningful progress. I refer to these individuals as **change champions**—team members who serve as catalysts for change, bridging the gap between new initiatives and team-wide adoption. By identifying their strengths and providing them with the right opportunities, executives can leverage change champions to support and encourage others, generating confidence across the organization during times of change.

Discovering and Leveraging Change Champions

Every successful change initiative requires harmony—a thoughtful mixture of those who anchor the team with stability (i.e., low change capacity) and those who propel it forward with adaptability (i.e., high change capacity). While all team members contribute unique strengths, discovering and strategically positioning individuals with high change capacity can amplify the impact of an initiative. Their readiness to new approaches helps bridge the gap between innovative ideas and practical execution.

Consider this example: a midsize technology firm is preparing to adopt new project management software across its departments. This transition is significant, as it replaces a system that has been in place for over a decade. Many employees, comfortable with the old software, are apprehensive about the learning curve of the new platform.

Enter Sarah, a team lead in the operations department who has consistently enjoyed exploring the possibilities of change. Rather than waiting for formal training sessions, she takes the initiative to explore the new software on her own. She dives into the new features, learning which could benefit the organization. In team meetings, she shares her insights, showcasing how certain features can streamline workflows and save time (capacity). When her teammates express hesitation about the new system, she acknowledges their worries and offers practical insights to ease the transition. Recognizing a need for additional support, she organizes an informal training session to guide her colleagues through the basics of the new software. Her awareness of teammates with lower change capacity moves her to implement these training sessions, using her influence and acquired knowledge to create a smooth transition process in incremental steps.

Sarah's proactive approach and willingness to help do not go unnoticed. Her enthusiasm for learning the new software gradually encourages more team members to engage with the platform. Sarah becomes the go-to person for questions, helping to build confidence across her department, creating momentum for sustainable change within the organization.

Strategies for Leveraging Change Champions:
- **Look for invisible influencers** - Sarah would be categorized as an invisible influencer. In the story, she exhibits influence within the team through actions rather than words or the weight of her title. To discover a Sarah on your team, notice who colleagues turn to for guidance, particularly in times of transition. These individuals are usually respected not only for their knowledge, but also for their willingness and encouragement to support others through change.

- **Recognize consistent initiative** - Change champions tend to be proactive, often taking the lead on exploring new ideas and processes before others do. Observe who consistently engages with new projects or actively contributes ideas during brainstorming sessions. This readiness often stems from a genuine interest rather than from a need for recognition.

- **Assign transformative projects** - Approach change champions with projects that leverage their strengths and align with bigger goals. Rather than viewing their role as honorary, treat it as an opportunity for meaningful contribution. Clearly communicate how their involvement can positively impact productivity and team morale, reinforcing their role in driving beneficial change within the organization.

- **Facilitate cross-functional collaboration** - Involve change champions in cross-departmental projects to leverage their adaptability and creativity, which often brings valuable insights. Cross-functional collaboration helps these individuals contribute to broader organizational goals, enhancing innovation across teams.

Supporting change champions with purpose-driven roles not only maximizes productivity but also strengthens a culture of adaptability and resilience. By integrating the different capacity types into organizational growth efforts, executives can harness these individual strengths to help teams remain adaptable, motivated, and ready for what's on the horizon.

Change Capacity and Leadership

It feels necessary to point out, it might seem that an entire team of high change capacity individuals would accelerate progress, but in reality, this often leads to missteps, change fatigue, and sometimes a lack of alignment. Without the counterbalance of thoughtful caution, offered by low change capacity team members, change can become disorganized rather than constructive. Conversely, a team composed entirely of low change capacity individuals may struggle to move forward, getting caught in cycles of over-analysis and hesitation.

Understanding the varied change capacities within your team is a leadership skill with lasting impact. Both high and low change capacity individuals contribute distinct, equally valuable strengths that, when combined, create a balanced and effective approach to navigating transitions. When leaders recognize and intentionally leverage these complementary strengths, they create transitions that are not only ambitious but also sustainable. Ultimately, this isn't about labeling team members; it's about positioning each individual where they contribute best. By integrating change capacity into your leadership approach, you create a team that is not only adaptable but also resilient.

"In a world of constant change, cultivating and leveraging change capacity isn't just an advantage—it's the foundation of resilience and progress." - Hilani Ellis

Self-Assessment

Answer yes or no to each question.

1. Do you actively assess each team member's capacity for handling transitions to ensure the right level of support?
2. Are you attentive to signs that indicate a team member may need additional support when navigating new processes or

initiatives?

3. Do you involve team members in sharing their thoughts on upcoming changes to better gauge readiness and potential obstacles?

4. Do you adapt your leadership approach based on the varying change capacities within your team to balance progress and stability?

5. Do you adjust communication and implementation strategies so both high and low change capacity team members remain engaged and productive?

6. Do you create space for reflection and feedback after major changes to strengthen future change readiness?

7. Do you leverage team members with higher change capacity to help support peers during challenging transitions?

Scoring and Guidance

More yes answers: You have a strong awareness of your team's change capacity levels. This understanding likely enables you to provide tailored support, creating a harmonious and adaptable team that is prepared for ongoing transitions.

More no answers: You have room for improvement in recognizing and supporting your team's varying change capacities. Focusing on observing team dynamics, seeking feedback, and providing customized support will help you create an environment that plays to the strengths of each team member.

Launch Pad

1. **Assess and support change readiness:** Regularly gauge how prepared your team is for upcoming transitions. Check

in with individuals to ensure responsibilities remain manageable and address capacity concerns before they impact progress. Offer adjustments or resources to help balance workload and maintain momentum.

2. **Embed a growth-oriented approach to change:** Frame change as a strategic advantage rather than a disruption. Reinforce adaptability by highlighting small wins and showcasing past successes. Encourage reflection on lessons learned to help team members build confidence in their ability to navigate change.

3. **Facilitate a team conversation on change capacity:** Before diving into change initiatives, lead a discussion on change capacity. Share your own experiences first to set the tone, then invite team members to reflect on their natural approach to change. Encourage them to identify how their strengths contribute to the team's success. To enhance the conversation, have everyone read this chapter beforehand. This helps create a shared understanding, allowing high and low change capacity individuals to appreciate each other's perspectives and work together more effectively.

CONDITIONING

Have you ever stopped to consider how much of your work style is shaped by default habits rather than intentional ones? Most of us operate on autopilot—executing tasks, meeting demands, and checking things off without questioning whether our current approach is the most effective. Because things are getting done, we assume our methods are working. When our routines feel efficient, it's easy to believe we're operating at full capacity. But what if those default habits are quietly limiting your capacity, effectiveness, and progress?

In Chapter 3, *Status Quo*, we explored the benefits of maintaining familiar systems as well as the advantages of adopting something new. But deciding to shift is only the first step. What happens after the choice is made? How do you ensure the shift takes hold, rather than becoming another fleeting attempt to work differently? That's where conditioning comes in.

At the individual level, conditioning plays a powerful role in shaping how we approach work, refine skills, and sustain productivity. The habits we repeat—both consciously and unconsciously—determine how we engage with tasks, respond to

CONDITIONING

challenges, and build momentum. While these tendencies provide structure, they can also create blind spots—leading us to rely on methods that may no longer serve us.

In Chapter 1, *Bending Time*, I introduced an exercise that required holding a plank for 60 seconds—not just as a physical challenge, but to help you recondition how you perceive time. Now, let's build on that idea with another exercise designed to highlight how conditioning evolves the way we work.

If you are able, grab a writing instrument and a piece of paper. With your nondominant writing hand, write your first name four times. If your name is five letters or less, write it five times.

When conducting leadership workshops, I ask participants to do this exercise at the beginning of our time together. The exercise is received with mixed emotions because it's fresh and isn't exhausting, sort of. The verbal reactions are usually humorous: *"Oh my gosh, this is going to be interesting," "I already know how mine is going to look,"* or *"I don't know if I want to do this"* (while exhibiting a playful smile). Mid-exercise, many participants stop to look at their neighbors' work. Some end up writing their name five times (without having to), motivated by a mix of frustration and a desire for visual perfection in their results. This conditioning exercise is powerful because it disrupts natural neural pathways, challenging the brain to expand its capacity by doing something unfamiliar—and likely uncomfortable.

Once completed, we showcase each person's 'artwork,' playfully grading their masterpieces on a scale from kindergarten to 2nd grade. Then, we go around the group to discuss how it felt and what insights emerged. During the discussion, many executives express discomfort with the task; some mention how they grew impatient (evident by the gradual decline in their writing quality with each attempt). A few, though, describe finding it enjoyable. The variety of reactions is always insightful, offering a glimpse into how individuals process unfamiliar tasks and adapt to discomfort.

Patience—or the lack of it—comes up every time. For those who experienced discomfort, we often trace it back to the concepts of change capacity from Chapter 5. Their interest or enjoyment affects their effort and patience levels. When participants feel less interested, they tend to grow more frustrated; when they experience enjoyment, they display greater patience. Overall, their feedback acts as a powerful indicator of each participant's capacity to engage in unfamiliar tasks and expand beyond what feels natural.

Understanding Conditioning

Conditioning is not commonly considered when discussing productivity and effectiveness, yet it plays a vital role in transforming intentional actions into quality habits that drive success. While training focuses on the "how-to" of tasks—equipping employees with immediate, actionable steps—conditioning turns those steps into second nature, solidifying habits that support continued progress. Just as with the writing exercise, doing something consistently—even when it feels uncomfortable—eventually leads to ease and fluency.

Tony Robbins, author, coach and speaker, once said, "It's not what we do once in a while that shapes our lives, but what we do consistently."[1] This quote applies to both sides of the conditioning process: reinforcing quality habits that drive progress and unlearning the tendencies that shape and reinforce undeserving

CONDITIONING

habits.

It's important to acknowledge that everyone, even the most seasoned executives, establish work habits over time that may no longer serve them or their goals. Familiar routines can feel efficient simply because they're comfortable, yet they often conceal inefficiencies that quietly limit progress. Skipping the conditioning process—where outdated habits are intentionally examined and remodeled—limits the opportunity to refine workflows and align daily actions with strategic priorities. When this process is overlooked, long-held habits remain unchallenged, even if they no longer serve the leader or the organization's broader goals.

Perhaps you've experienced days where you felt like you were constantly 'putting out fires'—addressing one urgent issue after another. While this cycle might create a false sense of capability, it ultimately fosters inefficiency, draining capacity, limiting the ability to achieve more meaningful outcomes. Without consistent reinforcement of quality habits, even the most deliberate efforts risk losing their impact, leaving executives and teams stuck in a reactive loop that undermines their long-term effectiveness. On the other hand, when new habits are thoughtfully conditioned, they begin to feel natural—reducing friction, increasing efficiency, and allowing leaders to operate with greater ease, clarity, and impact.

It's important to highlight that conditioning isn't limited to work habits—it's equally powerful in remodeling how we think, growing mental resilience. As discussed in Chapter 1, *Bending Time,* shifting from a mindset of time-scarcity to one of time-abundance doesn't just improve how tasks are executed—it redefines how priorities are set, steps are taken, and resources are allocated.

Conditioning in Action

To build upon the writing exercise offered earlier, and to help you visualize the impact of conditioning: imagine a 30-day challenge where you dedicated just 60 seconds each day to the writing exercise. By the end of the month, you'd likely see improvement, experience increased ease, and feel less frustration. This repetition builds muscle memory, strengthening neural pathways and making the task progressively easier and more automatic. As Benjamin Franklin said, "Tell me and I forget, teach me and I may remember, involve me and I learn."[2]

To illustrate the profound impact of conditioning, Michael Phelps, the most decorated Olympian of all time, provides a powerful real-world example. His success was not only a result of physical mastery but also the outcome of meticulous physical and mental conditioning. His coach, Bob Bowman, intentionally introduced challenges—such as one time stepping on Phelps' goggles before a race—to simulate high-pressure situations. Phelps' relentless conditioning activities enabled him to build extraordinary mental and physical resilience, an invaluable capacity builder for thriving in high-stakes environments.[3]

Conditioning, however, is not without its demands. Behind every achievement lies the effort and energy required to push beyond limits. Phelps himself has spoken in countless interviews about the physical exhaustion and mental strain his preparation required. This cost—the sacrifice of time, comfort, and capacity to pursue excellence—is what I like to call **capacity cost**.

For Phelps, capacity cost meant enduring physical stress and navigating unexpected challenges to cultivate an unshakable focus. But with every reinforcement of an activity—the conditioning—the capacity cost gradually decreased. For executives, capacity cost shows up in different ways: dedicating time to unlearn and remodel underserving habits, refining processes, or improving productivity through delegation.

Consider this: the first few times an executive resists the urge to jump in and solve a problem their team could handle, it may feel uncomfortable and even time-consuming to pause and let them figure it out. Yet, with repeated conditioning (practice), this new habit begins to stick—and team capacity grows alongside it. The executive gradually regains time, energy, and mental capacity. While the initial effort may feel like a high-capacity cost, it paves the way for long-term efficiency, stronger leadership, and sustainable growth.

This brings us to a pivotal choice: stick with a familiar process or habit that may feel effective in the moment but often lacks scalability and adaptability or invest in conditioning something new—which while initially demanding on your capacity, leads to expanded capacity and improved progress. Both paths have a capacity cost, but only one builds a foundation for greater productivity. So, why not choose the path that creates something better?

The Benefits of Conditioning

When you invest in conditioning and remodeling not just your work habits but also your mindset, the rewards enhance capacity and progress. By stepping away from the comfort of the familiar and embracing the potential of conditioning, you pave the way for meaningful growth that endures beyond the initial discomfort.

When I think about conditioning and discomfort, I'm reminded of one of my favorite clients (though truthfully, all my clients are my favorite—but this one was extra special). Let's call him Bob. Bob was the CEO of a well-known real estate development firm, originally founded by his father. He was what I like to call a "legacy executive"—my preferred term for seasoned leaders in the Boomer category. Bob came to me through a referral from a friend in the Young Presidents' Organization (YPO), someone I had worked with previously.

Bob's long-time executive assistant had recently retired, and a year prior, he had hired her replacement on his own. Unfortunately, that arrangement wasn't working. We met privately one Saturday for a two-hour conversation to discuss his needs, his vision for his role at this stage of his career, and what wasn't working with his current situation. During that meeting, one thing became abundantly clear: while the year was 2018, Bob's work style was rooted in an earlier era. He still relied heavily on dictation—recording his instructions on tape for his assistant to transcribe into emails, notes, and tasks.

We had established a professional yet warm rapport during our conversation, so I felt comfortable gently pushing back on his outdated work style. "Bob," I asked with a smile, "why aren't you using modern tools, like dictation-to-text apps or software?"

He grinned, laughed, and said, "Hilani, I'm too old to learn something new."

I leaned in slightly and replied, "Bob, you don't act your age, so the version of you I'm talking to right now is fully capable of learning something new. And trust me—you'll be excited afterward and, candidly, wonder why you didn't make the switch sooner." I added a playful wink for good measure.

He chuckled and said, "Maybe. Let's finish the search first."

The search was a success, and when Bob hired his new assistant, I shared one key piece of advice with her: make it a goal to transition Bob from his tape-recording ways to something more modern. She smiled, accepted the challenge, and I reminded Bob of our earlier conversation.

I kept close tabs on their progress—not just out of professional diligence but because I was selfishly eager for play-by-play updates on how Bob was adjusting to the conditioning phase of adopting a new work habit. About six months later, Bob and I reconnected. Sure enough, he admitted, "It was hard at first, but you were right. We've optimized the process, and we're better off for it. Thanks, Hilani."

By adopting conditioning as a strategic investment, executives can shift their focus from short-term strain to long-term gain. It's this mindset that pushes through discomfort and transforms even the smallest adjustments into powerful drivers of progress and success.

Conditioning and Productivity

As Bob's story illustrates, the conditioning investment led to a positive outcome—greater productivity. Productivity is top of mind for most executives, and one of the most common challenges I hear is, "Hilani, it's just faster if I do it myself." While this instinct may save time in the moment, it reinforces the status quo and limits opportunities for growth and capacity expansion for both the executive and their team. Delegation, when approached thoughtfully, is more than handing off tasks; it's about conditioning both the executive and their team member(s) to take incremental steps toward greater responsibility, enabling shared growth and expanded capacity across the board.

This process isn't instantaneous—it's a journey. As I often remind my clients, "When taking on something new, leverage patience, because *you're living it while you're learning it.*" Bob was living the new habit, while he was learning it. The same applies to those you lead. By actively seeking delegation opportunities, executives not only decrease the capacity cost tied to holding onto too much responsibility but increase both their own and their team's overall capacity to take on work collectively, strengthening both productivity and collaboration.

Consider this: What would it feel like to handle only 50% (or less) of a task that currently consumes significant capacity? Imagine the freedom this shift could bring—not just to your schedule but to your mental agility. Start by identifying one high-capacity-cost task and envision how delegating part of it could create room for more strategic activities. This activity not only sparks excitement about the possibilities ahead but also lays the groundwork for more intentional and sustainable delegation.

Increase Capacity Through Delegation

While it might feel instinctive to start delegation by choosing the person first, beginning with the task itself offers a clearer path forward. By identifying the task, you can evaluate its scope, break it into manageable components, and ensure it aligns with your team's strengths. This approach brings clarity to the delegation process and sets the stage for assigning it to the right person with purpose and confidence.

When it's time to identify the right team member, ask yourself: Is there someone eager to grow and ready to take on more responsibility? Are they equipped—or could they be equipped

CONDITIONING

with the right guidance—to handle both the foundational steps of the task and beyond? This initial phase of delegation is more than task allocation; it's about conditioning. Framing the delegation approach in this way ensures that both the team member and the process are set up for success, reinforcing quality habits that drive long-term efficiency and impact.

After identifying the task, the foundational steps, and the right team member, consider these next steps to integrate conditioning into the delegation process:

1. **Schedule shadow events -**

    a) Observe: Let the team member watch you perform the task. (You have to do it anyway.) Use this time to explain your thought process and reasoning behind each step, reinforcing the "why" as much as the "how".

    b) Practice: Swap roles, allowing them to take the lead while you observe, stepping in only to provide guidance. This builds their confidence and exposes them to the nuances of the task.

2. **Debrief after shadow events** - After each session, reflect together. What worked well? Where did they need more clarity? Share actionable tips and insights to reinforce their progress and address any gaps. This reflective dialogue not only strengthens their understanding of the task at hand but also conditions them for improved communication and problem-solving in future work activities.

3. **Gradually hand over ownership** - Once the delegation process feels comfortable for both you and the team member, allow them to take on more responsibility while maintaining

regular check-ins to provide support and feedback. These consistent touchpoints are critical to the conditioning process, ensuring alignment with the task's goals.

4. **Celebrate progress** - Recognize their questions, efforts, and milestones along the way. Celebrating small wins reinforces their confidence and commitment, creating a positive reinforcement loop for future tasks.

As noted in Chapter 3, *Status Quo*, Michael Karnjanaprakorn, former CEO of Skillshare, emphasized the importance of communication: "The biggest lesson I've learned as CEO is the art of overcommunicating. I'm constantly repeating the vision of the company to our team. When I thought I couldn't over communicate anymore, I would reiterate the vision again."[4] When it comes to delegation, overcommunicating the task's purpose and impact ensures that conditioning efforts build clarity, alignment, and progress. This approach transforms delegation into a dynamic tool for fostering growth, creating a foundation for future delegation.

From Individual to Team Conditioning

The next phase of delegation and conditioning moves beyond one-on-one development to encompass the entire team. While working closely with individual team members establishes trust and builds skills, expanding these principles team-wide ensures consistency and alignment. This approach also nurtures champions for progress—team members who actively embrace and promote the principles of delegation and conditioning, similar to the concept of change champions discussed in Chapter 5.

This shift from individual to collective focus fosters an environment where shared goals drive collaboration, allowing each member to contribute meaningfully. By embedding these conditioning practices into the team dynamic, leaders cultivate a foundation of trust and accountability that benefits the organization as a whole.

Here are key areas where conditioning enhances team outcomes:

1. **Establishing quality habits** - Setting and reinforcing quality habits through conditioning creates a shared foundation for effective teamwork. When executives consistently model and encourage quality habits, team members condition habits that align with desired outcomes, leading to increased reliability and capacity.

> *Example:* Consider a marketing team working toward the launch of a high-profile campaign. To condition effective, quality habits, the executive introduces a 15-minute daily "focus alignment" meeting where each team member shares *only* their top priority for the day. This activity helps the team maintain clarity, avoid overlapping efforts, and practice sticking to something new. If a topic unnecessarily joins the discussion, a revert to the meeting focus happens. Over time, the habit of aligning priorities fosters stronger collaboration, enhancing productivity.

2. **Communication conditioning** - Conditioning team members in communication practices enhances mutual understanding and efficiency. When team members are encouraged to use shared communication strategies, they create a more unified approach to dialogue, especially under pressure. This conditioning not only enhances clarity but also builds the capacity for effective collaboration during routine or high-stakes situations.

> *Example:* In a tech company, team members might use the 60-

second rule during meetings to consider thoughts before responding, leading to more thoughtful dialogue. Additionally, using the AEIOu Method during discussions helps team members understand each other's perspectives, fostering a shared language for innovating and executing. Initially introducing new communication tactics will take time, but the capacity cost of clarity in communication is worth the conditioning investment.

3. **Constructive feedback loops** - Conditioning team members to regularly seek and provide feedback on processes or situations builds a culture of continuous improvement, encouraging everyone to identify opportunities for refinement and innovation. Feedback loops centered on workflows or shared initiatives help teams align their efforts with broader goals while fostering a sense of collective ownership.

Example: During weekly team check-ins, a manager asks team members to highlight one aspect of a process or project that's working well and/or one area where adjustments could enhance efficiency and outcomes. This approach keeps the focus on systems rather than critiquing individuals. To encourage thoughtful responses, the manager might send an email prior to the meeting outlining the question, giving team members time to reflect and prepare. Over time, the repetitive nature of including this activity in meetings becomes conditioning in action—promoting greater collaboration and helping teams approach constructive initiatives with a solutions-oriented mindset.

4. **Performance Accountability** - Sometimes, conditioning is required to address ongoing challenges that impact both individual performance and team dynamics. When a team

member consistently underperforms or struggles to meet the demands of their role, it doesn't just affect their output—it can disrupt the team's overall capacity and alignment. Conditioning team members to embrace accountability fosters a culture where trust, reliability, and progress thrive. By addressing performance gaps constructively and setting clear expectations, executives can help team members grow into their roles and deliver meaningful contributions. This creates an environment where accountability becomes second nature, strengthening the team's ability to work cohesively and achieve shared goals.

Example: When a team member is struggling to meet expectations, the executive can address these gaps by fostering accountability in a constructive and supportive manner. Rather than immediately resorting to a Performance Improvement Plan (PIP)—a term often associated with discipline—you could instead leverage the Performance Enhancement Plan (PEP), an alternative method I developed. While the two approaches have similar objectives, the term "enhancement" shifts the focus toward growth and forward progress. It's a subtle but meaningful reframing that conditions the team member to see accountability as an opportunity rather than a reprimand.

Using a PEP allows the executive to help the team member take ownership of their responsibilities by offering guidance and clear benchmarks for success. This conditioning approach not only reinforces accountability but also fosters growth and strengthens the team's collective capacity to succeed. (Side note: As someone who was varsity cheer captain in high school, I can't resist mentioning the fun connection here—a pep rally was always about energizing the team, and that's exactly what a PEP aims to do in the workplace!)

It's important to remember, conditioning isn't just about creating individual habits—it's about fostering a collective mindset that amplifies team capacity and productivity. By establishing quality habits, shared communication frameworks, regular feedback, and accountability, leaders lay the groundwork for a culture that values evolution and adaptability.

The Enduring Value of Conditioning

As we've outlined in this chapter, conditioning creates immense value for executives, teams, and organizations. By remodeling work styles, reinforcing quality habits, and leveraging consistency, it serves as a strategic practice that transforms the way individuals and teams operate. When executives incorporate conditioning into their leadership approach, they set a standard of intentionality and growth that others naturally follow. This practice goes beyond productivity—it creates a culture where clarity, alignment, and adaptability flourish. Conditioning isn't about adding more to the workload; it's about embedding habits that make progress more achievable and sustainable. By making conditioning an integral part of your leadership style and company culture, you equip your team to excel today while also preparing them for what's next, fostering continuous growth and delivering sustained value.

"Conditioning yields remarkable outcomes." - *Hilani Ellis*

Self-Assessment

Answer yes or no to each question.

1. Do you regularly audit your work style to ensure your habits support your current goals and capacity needs?

CONDITIONING

2. Do you give yourself and your team enough time to condition new habits, allowing them to become second nature gradually?
3. Are you intentional about breaking tasks into smaller steps to make delegation and habit conditioning more approachable for your team?
4. Do you demonstrate patience and adaptability when introducing new habits or processes?
5. Do you involve your team in the conditioning process, helping them practice and refine habits that increase their capacity?
6. Do you encourage regular reflection on progress to ensure conditioning efforts stay aligned with long-term goals?
7. Do you actively identify and phase out outdated habits that no longer support greater productivity or strategic focus?

Scoring and Guidance

More yes answers: You are actively embracing conditioning as a tool to build capacity for yourself and your team. Your approach reflects patience, intentionality, and a commitment to fostering progress that aligns with long-term goals.

More no answers: Your responses highlight opportunities to deepen your conditioning efforts. By focusing on small, deliberate adjustments and involving your team in the process, you can build habits that strengthen both individual and collective capacity over time.

Launch Pad

1. **Align priorities together:** Host a quick weekly check-in with

your team to align on *one shared goal* for the week. Discuss how individual contributions connect to the larger objective. This practice conditions clarity, reinforces alignment, and ensures everyone is working toward meaningful progress.

2. **Create a reflection ritual:** At the end of the week or a project milestone, ask your team to share one success and one lesson learned. This simple practice reinforces the habit of continuous improvement and conditions a growth-focused mindset.

3. **Lead by example:** Pick one of your own work habits you believe would benefit from an update. Disclose the habit to your team and how you're going to approach the remodeling. This invites accountability and demonstrates how investing in conditioning can lead to meaningful improvements over time.

WORK-LIFE HARMONY

My journey with capacity-focused leadership revealed a universal truth: one of the greatest challenges leaders face—right behind scaling businesses—is balancing work and life in a way that is both impactful and fulfilling. This challenge isn't limited to those at the top; it's one that resonates throughout entire organizations, shaping individual productivity, employee experiences, and team culture. Over time, it influences broader outcomes, such as team strength and employee retention—topics we'll delve into later in this chapter.

For many, striving for balance between work and life feels like an endless struggle—a goal that almost always seems just out of reach. It's a daily juggling act that leaves us feeling stretched thin. But what if balance isn't the pursuit? Through my journey, I've discovered a more worthwhile aspiration: work-life harmony.

So, what exactly is harmony? Unlike balance, which implies equal distribution and stability, harmony focuses on integration and flow. It's about positioning the elements of work and life in a way that allows them to complement—rather than compete with—each other. By recognizing this fluidity, harmony offers a practical, adaptable approach to managing the ever-changing demands of modern life.

Imagine this: we're in a high school science classroom, and I'm standing at the front of the class behind a lab table, holding two 5-ounce glass jars, one in each hand. Each jar is filled with sand—one representing work, the other personal life. In front of me stands a balance scale, its arms stretched wide, each holding a plate ready to weigh the jars' contents. Each grain of sand represents a task, an obligation, or a moment of joy. While the jars appear to hold equal amounts of sand, we all know life's demands rarely split evenly. One jar almost always outweighs the other, pulling our focus disproportionately.

As I slowly pour sand from both jars onto the scale plates, the grains cascade out, forming tiny dunes on either side. The scale sways back and forth, attempting to stabilize, but it never quite finds equilibrium (balance).

This simple experiment reveals an important truth: balance, in its rigid form, isn't just challenging—it's impossible. In real life, it looks like this: a work emergency might send a heavy stream of sand tipping the scale toward professional demands. Similarly, a family or personal matter could distribute more sand toward personal priorities. The dynamic movement of the sand mirrors the evolving nature of our lives, underscoring why striving for perfect balance often leaves us frustrated.

As illustrated in the experiment, the traditional concept of work-life balance suggests a perfect equilibrium where professional and personal demands coexist without conflict. Yet, this notion is inherently flawed because it fails to account for the inevitable shifts and pressures of real life. Instead of chasing balance, embracing work-life harmony equips us to navigate these fluctuations with intention and flexibility.

Work-Life Harmony in Action

When facilitating work-life harmony workshops, I introduce in the first 15-minutes a simple, yet thought-provoking question: "What would you do with three extra hours in your work week?" Occasionally, the room breaks into a knowing laugh, as someone inevitably voices the common abstain: "How in the world am I going to find three hours?" That moment of laughter often serves as a shared acknowledgment of our collective time constraints, but it also opens the door to a shift in mindset.

Consider this: with simple back-of-the-envelope math, saving seven 5-minute intervals each day would yield you an extra three hours over the course of a typical work week. This seemingly small adjustment—shaving off moments of inefficiency or rethinking how you approach delegation—can lead to a significant increase in capacity and productivity.

Not surprisingly, the three-hour question prompts a range of intriguing responses. Some participants want more sleep, others hope to start working out again, spend more time with family, pick up old hobbies, or, as one executive shared, "Start writing a book." After each executive shares their response, we discuss them deeper as a group. I recall a particular exchange with a CEO—let's call her Jeannette. When I asked what she would do with three extra hours, Jeannette said she'd like to start working out again. "That's great, Jennette," I replied, "What would that look like in action?" I encouraged her to elaborate. Jeannette hesitated, her expression light but slightly cautious, before responding with a good-humored tone: "Well, Hilani, start working out," she said, adding a playful 'duh' expression. I smiled back and respectfully pressed further: "In the morning, at home, in a gym, lifting weights, running, spinning, yoga, Pilates—what does working out again look like to you?" This time, Jeannette paused, nodded, and offered a smile of recognition, realizing the nudge behind my challenge. Around the room, other executives were nodding along, a clear signal that they too understood the importance of being specific.

The Power of Specificity

Having specificity is crucial. Visualizing the exact steps needed to achieve any goal is the key to taking action. Just as Tiger Woods, one of the greatest golfers of all time, visualizes the ball landing exactly where he wants it before he swings, we must think through our aspirations in detail, assigning clarity and focus to our plans. Specificity is what turns abstract desires into actionable objectives.[1]

Consider planning a trip. You start with a destination in mind—somewhere exciting, relaxing, or inspiring. Then, you figure out logistics: flights, accommodations, and activities. Each intentional choice builds momentum, shaping the experience you hope to achieve. In the same way, specificity transforms vague desires into achievable steps, propelling you toward the desired outcome.

Marc Randolph, co-founder of Netflix, exemplifies this well. His dedication and specificity to Tuesday night date nights with his wife isn't just a routine; it's a deliberate act of harmony.[2] By prioritizing quality time, he strengthens his relationship and proves that work-life integration is achievable, even in high-pressure environments. Additionally, by being unavailable every

Tuesday night, he sends a clear message to his team about the importance of focusing on work and personal life.

In this example, harmony starts with the individual and with intention (specificity). Executives who embrace this approach don't just set goals—they expand their capacity to design lives where work and personal priorities complement each other, even amid demands.

Designing Your Personal Harmony

Harmony isn't a one-size-fits-all concept. It's deeply personal, shaped by your values, goals, and the rhythm of your life. Just like Jeannette gained clarity by adding specificity to her working out goal, designing your own harmony plan starts with focused reflection. Fortunately, creating your plan doesn't require a massive overhaul or endless preparation. Your first step in a few steps process is simple: set aside 30–45 uninterrupted minutes to identify *core* commitment(s) you wish to focus on next week—what we'll call your **anchors**. Your anchors ground you in the priorities that help you intentionally integrate work and life, creating a foundation for harmony. Investing this time is a rewarding activity as it sets the tone for how you'll navigate your work and life with greater clarity and purpose.

During the first step, and to help you identify your anchors, use the simple, yet powerful question from the workshop session:

Step 1 - The 3-Hour Question

If you had three extra hours in your work week (remember, that's just seven 5-minute intervals each day, during a work week), what would you do?

It's important to note, the actual remodeling efforts required to reclaim those three hours is a separate process. For now, this question helps you identify what you would do with that time, allowing you to approach your week with that focus in mind—even before the time is fully available. You're leveraging the question to reveal what produces the greatest impact for you and those around you, allowing work-life harmony to start taking shape. Feel free to dream a little, making a long list of options. For some, the answer might be spending more time with family, reigniting a hobby, or focusing on strategy. For others, it might be tackling a long-ignored project or becoming more hands-on with their team. An executive once shared with me that he wished for more time to walk the floor of their manufacturing plant—a simple act that kept him connected to his staff and operations. It's fair to assume that spending this time, and investing it this way, could lead to many positive outcomes.

Step 2 - Leveraging the Anchor Method

The Anchor Method is a system I developed to help executives and teams create sustainable plans that drive productivity, improve delegation, enhance strategic focus, and foster work-life harmony. It centers on devoting capacity to your anchors, guiding a purposeful and impactful week. Anchors aren't just tasks; they're the core priorities that ensure your focus and capacity are directed with intention.

From your list to the three-hour question, build a list of 1-3 anchors that will serve as your foundation in the coming week. Oftentimes, the anchors are non-negotiables that bring stability and purpose to your work and life integration pursuit. For ambitious executives, feel comfortable with one anchor. That may be all you need to achieve work-life harmony that week.

Sample anchors:

1. Attending your child's sports practice on Thursday.
2. Dedicating 30-minutes to strategic thinking three times.
3. Find one meeting that can be reduced in duration.
4. Get in three short walks each day.

To share, the Anchor Method isn't just something I recommend—it's a method I use every week. With my assistant, we use the Anchor Method to heighten our focus and maintain our capacity. One of my recurring anchors has been dedicating time to finishing this book—a rewarding but demanding pursuit. Other anchors might be focused on unique client and candidate activities or brainstorming a new workshop concept. While our to-do list is seemingly endless, the anchors are intentional and purposeful, standing out as the core priorities that keep us grounded each week.

Because my assistant is fully immersed in the day-to-day business activities—and to save me from juggling yet another decision and task—she identifies our anchors every Friday for the upcoming week. Additionally, we set monthly anchors to maintain momentum on larger goals, like planning a new initiative or dedicating time for business outreach.

These anchors not only clarify where our focus should go each week but also act as a filter, helping us eliminate distractions and evaluate opportunities. A filtering question we ask is, "How does this fit with our weekly or monthly anchors?" This constant check-in keeps us grounded and intentional.

The beauty of the Anchor Method lies in its simplicity and flexibility. It's not about striving for a fixed plan; it's about creating a clear and harmonious path forward—one that feels achievable and purposeful. By intentionally choosing and honoring your anchors, you expand your capacity, maintain focus, and have a higher chance of cultivating a sense of harmony between your work and personal life.

Step 3 - Commit to Your Anchors

Once your anchors are identified, you'll need a guiding principle to help you honor them. You might lean on the prior filtering question, or you can try one of my other favorites: the **Hard Yes Rule**. Simply put: If it isn't a hard yes, then it must be a no. Of course, not every decision can be black and white—realities like urgent demands or unforeseen circumstances may require flexibility. The Hard Yes Rule isn't about being rigid; it's about making intentional choices.

As we discussed in the prior chapter, capacity is a precious resource, and every choice carries a capacity cost—the effort, energy, and focus required to manage your commitments and stay aligned with your anchors. The Hard Yes Rule helps you evaluate requests, obligations, and distractions through this lens, ensuring your capacity is directed where it's most impactful that week.

For example:

1. A spontaneous meeting request. If it doesn't directly support your anchors for the week, decline, delegate it, or suggest handling it over email.
2. A project idea from your team. If it's valuable but not urgent, acknowledge its importance and flag it as a potential anchor for next week. This ensures it gets the attention it deserves without disrupting the current week's focus.

3. A last-minute invitation on Monday for a coffee date on Thursday. If it aligns with a larger anchor to prioritize relationships, go for it. If it conflicts with a non-negotiable like a one-on-one meeting or personal activity, it's okay to politely decline and propose a future date.

By using the filtering question or rule, you stay focused on what drives progress and fulfillment while maintaining the flexibility to adapt as needed. This strategy keeps your efforts aligned with your anchors and reinforces your pursuit of work-life harmony. By prioritizing harmony, individuals cultivate a resilient capacity that benefits not only their own lives but also the lives of their families, teams, and organizations.

Work-Life Harmony and Employee Experience

Leaving behind the outdated notion of work-life balance to embrace work-life harmony is one of the most impactful ways executives can champion their teams, elevating the employee experience. By adopting a work-life harmony mindset, executives reset how employees view their relationship with work, fostering a renewed sense of engagement and purpose. Prioritizing workplace alignment with employees' needs can strengthen collaboration and trust, demonstrating that the organization values its people by actively honoring boundaries.

The *American Psychological Association's October 2023 Work in America Survey* highlights the importance of respecting boundaries between work and personal time. According to the survey, 95% of workers consider it very or somewhat important to work for an organization that upholds these boundaries.[3] This finding emphasizes the need for intentional planning that harmonizes the employee experience with life well-being goals, all while supporting meaningful progress for both employees and the organization.

This alignment between employee well-being and organizational success isn't achieved through standalone programs or surface-level perks—it's cultivated through deliberate cultural shifts that prioritize how work gets done, how leadership models healthy boundaries, and how teams are motivated to contribute without sacrificing their personal well-being.

A 2024 *Harvard Business Review* article, "*Why Workplace Well-Being Programs Don't Achieve Better Outcomes*," reveals that programs often falter when they rely on generic solutions.[4] The key to enhancing the employee experience relies on embracing the individuality of your organization's values, creating initiatives that reflect its unique design. By addressing workplace well-being thoughtfully and collaboratively, leaders can lay the groundwork for work-life integration that not only supports employees but also energizes the organization toward sustainable progress. Now, this doesn't mean accommodating every individual preference or solving every personal challenge. Instead, it's about introducing a perspective on work-life harmony that aligns with the organization's values and priorities. For instance, simply announcing a shift from the traditional concept of work-life balance to work-life harmony can spark curiosity and signal a fresh direction. This shift requires no immediate investment but offers an opportunity to invite input, gather feedback, and shape a shared understanding of how work-life harmony can take shape within your organization. Think of this as a guiding principle—clear, concise, and actionable—that reflects the organization's dedication to supporting its people while pursuing company goals.

To illustrate how leaders can implement practical strategies for fostering work-life harmony across their teams, let's consider this example: Beth, a manager at a midsized tech company, used the Anchor Method to help her team harmonize high-priority work with realistic capacity during a high-stakes product launch. By aligning individual tasks with shared priorities and encouraging intentional focus, Beth not only kept the team on track but also helped them protect space for thoughtful work, collaboration, and personal commitments—creating a culture where work-life harmony felt achievable, even during high-pressure periods.

Step 1 - Identifying Team Anchors

During a weekly planning session, Beth introduces the Anchor Method. Then, follows up with a question to the group: *"If we/you could focus on [x] number of core priorities this week to make the biggest impact, what would they be, and why?"* The team brainstorms together and identifies the following anchors:

1. Finalize the marketing style guide specifics for the new product launch.
2. Review old product launch notes to learn what worked and what didn't.
3. Block time to attend an industry leader webinar to gain insights on upcoming trends associated with launching the new product.

Step 2 - Aligning Tasks to Anchors

With the anchors defined, Beth assigns them based on team strengths. She also encourages team members to align their individual tasks with these priorities. This ensures that everyone's efforts contribute directly to the team's anchors for the week.

For example:

- The graphic designer schedules time to finalize the visuals for the marketing style guide, collaborating with a colleague to provide fresh eyes before submitting, ensuring the layout is accurate and on point.
- The content writer dedicates time to reviewing old product launch notes and materials.
- Beth attends the industry-specific webinar and prepares a concise brief summarizing the most relevant insights. She plans to share this with the team at their next meeting, helping refine the overall approach and incorporate best practices into the launch strategy.

Step 3 - The Hard Yes Rule

Beth introduces the Hard Yes Rule to help the team protect their capacity while adapting to the dynamic pace of work. The rule isn't about slowing things down or adding rigidity; it's about ensuring that every task aligns with the team's established core commitments—anchors—for the week. If a new task doesn't directly support the week's anchors or align with their individual goals, they deprioritize it or find a creative solution.

For example:

- When a colleague from another department requests an unscheduled meeting for later that day, the team member responds with an email resolution or schedules a brief call later in the week to avoid disrupting their current flow and focus.
- The graphic designer receives a request for additional visuals for another project at the eleventh hour. Rather than taking on

the task immediately, he consults with Beth to evaluate its alignment with the week's anchors. Together, they determine whether it can be deferred or incorporated without compromising the predetermined flow.

- A team member is invited to contribute to an unrelated initiative. While acknowledging its potential value, they provide a quick initial response and agree on a timeline for a deeper review the following week, ensuring it doesn't pull them away from their anchors.

By applying the Hard Yes Rule, Beth's team effectively manages unexpected requests and prioritizes other tasks alongside their weekly anchors without losing focus. This approach keeps the team adaptable in a fast-moving work environment while remaining aligned with their anchors. At the end of the week, Beth leads a brief reflection to celebrate progress, share insights, and adjust the next week's anchors based on the product launch's evolving needs.

These reflective moments reinforce focus and foster shared accountability and purpose. As discussed in Chapter 6, conditioning requires patience and the willingness to live and learn through the process. While it may not feel seamless initially, consistent use of the Anchor Method creates a rhythm of progress, transforming how teams approach their work and goals together. Imagine if the whole organization used the Anchor Method?

As James Clear explains in his book *Atomic Habits,* "It takes an average of 66 days to form a new habit."[5] This highlights the importance of persistence in integrating new habits into the team's workflow. Over time, these efforts make the new habits second nature, strengthening the team's capacity to navigate work and life. As these habits take root, they not only enhance individual and team performance but also contribute to a workplace culture that prioritizes alignment and shared goals—a critical factor in improving retention and reducing turnover.

Work-Life Harmony and Workplace Capacity

From conversations with countless CEOs and human resources professionals, it's clear that staying ahead of employee turnover remains a persistent challenge—one that consistently ranks among the top five concerns for employers. Time and again, I hear leaders searching for strategies that are both impactful and straightforward to implement—approaches that foster an engaging and fulfilling employee experience. A 2024 *Harvard Business Review* article, *"Why Employees Quit,"* confirms their challenges while identifying key drivers of turnover, including lack of recognition, poor work-life balance, and limited autonomy—issues that a work-life harmony culture is uniquely positioned to address.[6]

Implementing a work-life harmony approach might feel daunting, especially with an already full platter. However, the cost of inaction is far greater. According to the *Why Employees Quit* article, replacing an employee costs a company an average of 6 to 8 months of the departing employee's salary. For instance, replacing an employee earning $62,000 annually could cost between $31,000 and $41,000. These figures don't even account for the toll on morale, productivity, or the added strain placed on remaining team members, which can further disrupt progress.

Faced with these challenges, what's the right course of action to not only sustain but expand workplace capacity and improve the employee experience? This book outlines several low- to no-cost strategies—such as fostering work-life harmony through intentional planning, adopting the Anchor Method, or embracing new, meaningful habits—that can serve as a starting point. Additionally, employers might explore flexible work schedules, which have consistently shown positive impacts on both employee satisfaction and organizational performance.

Flexibility isn't just a buzzword—it's a practical, capacity-enhancing approach to reducing turnover, boosting morale, and sustaining productivity. A CNBC article, *"Win-win-win: Three-day hybrid work week is a success,"* highlights how hybrid schedules can reduce resignations by as much as one-third while maintaining or even improving employee performance and satisfaction.[7] This insight is reinforced by countless conversations I've had with executives, many of whom confirm that embracing flexibility leads to stronger work-life harmony.

Fostering Work-Life Harmony

The takeaway is clear: employees increasingly value work-life harmony, and employers stand to gain significantly by fostering it. By intentionally integrating work-life harmony into your company's culture, you expand capacity—both individual and organizational—creating opportunities for greater alignment, collaboration, and capacity. Start by experimenting with thoughtful changes that reflect your current, unique culture, actively involving your team in shaping new initiatives. The process doesn't have to be perfect—it simply needs to prioritize purpose and progress. With this mindset, you can create a workplace where capacity increases, talent is retained, and harmony drives collective success.

"Pursuing work-life harmony results in sustainable work-life

CAPACITY: THE NEW ADVANTAGE

integration" - Hilani Ellis

Self-Assessment

Answer yes or no to each question.

1. Do you intentionally set aside time for activities that recharge your energy, such as physical activity, personal time, or hobbies?
2. Do you regularly set aside time for strategic thinking to align your goals with your weekly objectives?
3. Does your daily and weekly routine support both your professional responsibilities and personal well-being?
4. Do you actively engage your team in discussions to identify ways their work can better support their individual work-life needs?
5. Do you encourage your team to align their efforts with shared goals in a way that respects their capacity and well-being?
6. Does your organization currently offer a culture that supports work-life integration through tangible actions or policies?
7. Do you regularly assess and adjust workplace policies to ensure they meet the evolving needs of your employees?

Scoring and Guidance

More yes answers: You're fostering work-life harmony and effectively managing your priorities. Continue building on these practices to sustain your well-being and inspire your team.
More no answers: Consider small but impactful adjustments to align your commitments more harmoniously. Focus on areas where you can reclaim capacity and create a more sustainable

routine for both you and your team.

Launch Pad

1. **Increase your capacity:** Imagine reclaiming three extra hours in your work week. What would you focus on? Whether it's personal fulfillment or professional growth, be specific about the impact this time could provide. Use this vision to inspire actionable changes that enhance both your capacity and productivity.

2. **Leverage the Anchor Method for individual and team alignment:** Consider adopting the Anchor Method as a resource to define both personal and team priorities. Encourage individuals to identify their weekly anchors that drive focus and impact. Then, in collaborative sessions, align anchors with the team's broader objectives.

3. **Make harmony a leadership practice:** As a leader, model the behaviors that reflect work-life harmony. Use specificity to identify clear boundaries, communicate transparently about priorities, and celebrate efforts that align with team goals. By embodying these principles, you set the tone for a workplace culture that values harmony and progress.

CAPACITY: THE NEW ADVANTAGE

THE DASH

Imagine standing with me around 6:30am on a cloudless June morning. The sun is rising in the East, casting a golden glow over the landscape. The temperature is a crisp 68 degrees, perfect for quiet reflection. We are standing on freshly manicured grass, the morning dew still glistening. Majestic trees line the horizon, their leaves gently rustling in the early morning breeze. As you look off into the distance, you see rows and rows of white headstones, perfectly aligned. Each stone represents a fallen soldier, a life that served its country. We are at Arlington National Cemetery, a place steeped in history and majestic reflection. Each headstone bears a name, a start year, and a concluding year, separated by a dash. This simple dash represents the entirety of that person's life, the choices they made, the impact they had, and the legacy they left behind. This poignant symbol, the dash, is what we will focus on in this final chapter. Just like those who rest at Arlington, each of us has a dash that represents our own legacy. It is the culmination of our decisions, actions, and the influence we leave behind. As leaders, your dash is not just a mark between two dates, but a testament to your life's work and the lives you've touched.

Reflecting on the poem "The Dash" by Linda Ellis (available to read after this chapter), we understand that the value of our lives isn't defined by the years themselves, but by what we do with the time in between.[1] The dash is a reminder to live fully, to lead with intent, and to make a meaningful contribution. In this short chapter, we will review the key principles from the previous chapters—Bending Time, Decision Fatigue, Status Quo, Risk

Reward, Change Capacity, Conditioning, and Work-Life Harmony—to illustrate how they collectively contribute to building a lasting legacy, your dash. By understanding and applying the concepts discussed, you can craft a life and career that is both successful and impactful.

Building a Leadership Legacy and Brand

Your leadership brand is the story of your dash. It's what you represent, how you approach challenges, and the influence you leave behind. Throughout this book, we've explored principles that lay the foundation for a life and career driven by purpose and built on capacity. Each principle contributes to shaping a dash that reflects integrity, adaptability, and a commitment to exceptionalism.

- **Bending Time** reminds us that time is fixed, but capacity is flexible. By maximizing our resources, energy, and focus, we ensure our dash reflects intention and presence rather than a reactive pursuit of tasks.

- Managing **Decision Fatigue** equips us with the strategies to make choices aligned with our values, helping us avoid the erosion of focus that can dilute our leadership brand.

- Challenging the **Status Quo** underscores a commitment to innovation and growth. A dash that embraces evolution, motivates others to question norms and pursue progress courageously.

- Considering **Risk Reward** strengthens your ability to act decisively, blending courage with caution. Pursuing both risk and reward effectively paves the way for growth and innovation that move beyond our immediate influence.

CAPACITY: THE NEW ADVANTAGE

- **Change Capacity** reminds us that the ability to adapt to new challenges is essential for impactful leadership. Expanding our capacity for change signals both growth and adaptability, allowing us to lead with resilience and intention. Leaders who leverage change capacity insights can inspire their teams to move forward confidently, embracing adaptability in an evolving world.

- **Conditioning** reinforces that consistent effort and building quality habits shape highly impactful work styles. Through conditioning, we develop thoughtful responses and disciplined habits that become second nature. This steady reinforcement of proactive practices defines our character and strengthens our legacy, demonstrating our commitment to continued improvement.

- **Work-Life Harmony** emphasizes the importance of multiple factors when considering well-being. A harmonious approach ensures our dash tells a story of fulfilled commitments, both personal and professional, rather than one dominated solely by work pursuits.

Building a Legacy of Lasting Influence

Ultimately, your dash reflects the culture you foster, the people you inspire, and the lives you touch. Leadership isn't merely (only) about achieving professional milestones; it's about leaving behind a legacy that others admire and aspire to carry forward. As you reflect on building your dash and legacy, ask yourself:

What story will my dash tell?

Will it inspire others to lead with purpose, resilience, and positive energy?

THE DASH

Will it reflect an unwavering commitment to adaptability, enhanced capacity, and evolution?

The decisions you make today shape the legacy you leave. Each choice, conversation, and commitment build a leadership brand that influences well into the future. As you step forward, remember that the story of your dash is still being written. Commit to a life of aspirations, positive influence, and fulfillment. Leave a legacy that serves as a beacon for others—a legacy that makes the world a better place.

"May your dash inspire others to reach higher, live fully, and lead with passion." - Hilani Ellis

Cheers to your Dash.

Now What?

www.HilaniEllis.com/capacity-book-resources

POEM

The Dash – Poem by Linda Ellis

I read of a man who stood to speak
at the funeral of a friend.
He referred to the dates on the tombstone
from the beginning…to the end.

He noted that first came the date of birth
and spoke the following date with tears,
but he said what mattered most of all
was the dash between those years.

For that dash represents all the time
that they spent alive on earth.
And now only those who loved them
know what that little line is worth.

For it matters not, how much we own,
the cars…the house…the cash.
What matters is how we live and love
and how we spend our dash.

So, think about this long and hard.
Are there things you'd like to change?
For you never know how much time is left
that can still be rearranged.

If we could just slow down enough
to consider what's true and real
and always try to understand
?the way other people feel.

And be less quick to anger
and show appreciation more
and love the people in our lives

like we've never loved before.

If we treat each other with respect
and more often wear a smile,
remembering that this special dash
might only last a little while.

So, when your eulogy is being read,
with your life's actions to rehash…
would you be proud of the things they say
about how you spent YOUR dash?

NOTES

What is Capacity?

1. Merriam-Webster.com Dictionary, s.v. "capacity," Accessed. (March 6, 2025). https://www.merriam-webster.com/dictionary/capacity.

Chapter 1: Bending Time

1. Droit-Volet, Sylvie, and Sandrine, Gil. "The time-emotion paradox." Philosophical transactions of the Royal Society of London. Series B, Biological sciences. (July 12, 2009). https://pmc.ncbi.nlm.nih.gov/articles/PMC2685815/

2. Yoo, Jeeun et al. "Comparison of Speech Rate and Long-Term Average Speech Spectrum between Korean Clear Speech and Conversational Speech." Journal of audiology & otology vol. 23,4 (July 20, 2019).

NOTES

https://pmc.ncbi.nlm.nih.gov/articles/PMC6773961/

3. Sapna. "Motivational Monday: For Every Minute Spent Organizing, An Hour Is Earned." The Teaching Cove. (July 10, 2017). https://www.teachingcove.com/motivate/every-minute-spent-organizing/

Chapter 2: Decision Fatigue

1. Hoomans, Dr. Joel. "35,000 Decisions: The Great Choices of Strategic Leaders." The Leading Edge. (March 20, 2015). https://go.roberts.edu/leadingedge/the-great-choices-of-strategic-leaders

2. Graff, Frank. "How Many Decisions Do We Make In One Day?" PBS North Carolina. (August 13, 2021). https://www.pbsnc.org/blogs/science/how-many-decisions-do-we-make-in-one-day/

3. Bezos, Jeff. "Jeff Bezos explains what it means to disagree and commit." Startup Archive. (December 16, 2023). https://www.startuparchive.org/p/jeff-bezos-explains-what-it-means-to-disagree-and-commit

Chapter 3: Status Quo

1. Godin, Seth. "Seth Godin: Master of Marketing." Financial Brand Forum. (March 7, 2025). https://financialbrandforum.com/seth-godin/

2. SpaceX. "Falcon 9." Accessed. (March 6, 2025). https://www.spacex.com/vehicles/falcon-9/

3. Oberoi, Sanjay. "The Evolution of Netflix: From DVD

Rentals to Global Streaming Leader." Seat11a. (December 3, 2024). https://seat11a.com/blog-the-evolution-of-netflix-from-dvd-rentals-to-global-streaming-leader/

4. Nadella, Satya, and London, Simon. "CEO Satya Nadella talks about innovation, disruption, and organizational change." McKinsey & Company. (April 3, 2018). https://www.mckinsey.com/industries/technology-media-and-telecommunications/our-insights/microsofts-next-act

5. Hinssen, Peter. "How Mary Barra resurrected General Motors." NexxWorks. (February 25, 2020). https://www.nexxworks.com/blog/how-mary-barra-resurrected-general-motors

6. Sofield, Deb. "'If you want something new, you have to stop doing something old.' Peter F. Drucker." Medium. (November 13, 2018). https://medium.com/@debsofield/if-you-want-something-new-you-have-to-stop-doing-something-old-peter-f-drucker-3ae509605b4f

7. Ewenstein, Boris, and Smith, Wesley, and Sologar, Ashvin. "Changing change management." (July 1, 2015). https://www.mckinsey.com/featured-insights/leadership/changing-change-management

8. Karnjanaprakorn, Michael. "Golden Rule of Managing Up." Skillshare Writings. Medium. (March 11, 2015). https://medium.com/skillshare-team/golden-rule-of-managing-up-b5d795eb862f

NOTES

Chapter 4: Risk Reward

1. Luna, Wilson. "Sara Blakely: Entrepreneur Who Turned $5,000 into a Billion-Dollar Spanx Empire." (October 2, 2024). https://www.wilsonluna.com/post/sara-blakely-story-spanx-story

2. Makinson, Rachel. "How Spanks Founder Sarah Blakely Created A Billion-Dollar Brand." CEO Today Magazine. (October 28, 2021). https://www.ceotodaymagazine.com/2021/10/how-spanx-founder-sara-blakely-created-a-billion-dollar-brand/

Chapter 5: Change Capacity

1. "'I'd rather quit': Study shows how CEOs really feel about transformation projects." Orgvue. (November 21, 2024). https://www.orgvue.com/resources/articles/id-rather-quit-study-shows-how-ceos-really-feel-about-transformation-projects/?

Chapter 6: Conditioning

1. Hanlon, Renee. "75 Inspiring Tony Robbins Quotes To Keep You Moving Forward." Parade. (November 16, 2024). https://parade.com/living/tony-robbins-quotes

2. Franklin, Benjamin. "Tell me and I forget, teach me and I may remember, involve me and I learn." Brainy Quote. (March 7, 2025). https://www.brainyquote.com/quotes/benjamin_franklin_383997

3. Shrivastava, Tilak. "From Goggle Mishap to Gold Medal: How 'What-If' Training Transformed Phelps at

the 2008 Olympics." Medium. (October 2, 2023). https://tilak.medium.com/from-goggle-mishap-to-gold-medal-how-what-if-training-transformed-phelps-at-the-2008-olympics-9c36715790bc

4. Karnjanaprakorn, Michael. "Why you need to over-communicate." World Economic Forum. (March 24, 2015). https://www.weforum.org/stories/2015/03/why-you-need-to-over-communicate/

Chapter 7: Work-Life Harmony

1. "Tiger Woods Putting Ball Position." Golf Hype. (December 13, 2023). https://thegolfhype.com/tiger-woods-putting-ball-position/

2. Tamta, Roshni. "'Staying married to the same woman': Netflix co-founder Marc Randolph shares his definition of success." My nation. (May 30, 2024). https://www.mynation.com/world/-staying-married-to-the-same-woman-netflix-co-founder-marc-randolph-shares-his-definition-of-success-rtm-seab4v

3. "2023 Work in America Survey: Workplaces as engine of psychological health and well-being." American Psychological Association. Accessed (March 5, 2025). https://www.apa.org/pubs/reports/work-in-america/2023-workplace-health-well-being

4. Croft, Jazz, and Parks, Acacia, and Whillans, Ashley. "Why Workplace Well-Being Programs Don't Achieve Better Outcomes." Harvard Business Review. (October 18, 2024). https://hbr.org/2024/10/why-workplace-well-being-programs-dont-achieve-better-outcomes

NOTES

5. Clear, James. "Atomic Habits: Tiny Changes, Remarkable Results." Penguin Random House. 2018.
6. Bernstein, Ethan, and Horn, Michael B., and Moesta, Bob. "Why Employees Quit." Harvard Business Review. (Magazine, November - December 2024). https://hbr.org/2024/11/why-employees-quit
7. Ginsky, Kaya. "'Win-win-win': Three-day hybrid work week is a success, largest study to date published in Nature says." CNBC. (June 14, 2024). https://www.cnbc.com/2024/06/14/three-day-hybrid-work-week-is-success-study-published-in-nature-says.html

Chapter 8: The Dash

1. Ellis, Linda. "The Dash." Best Poems Encyclopedia. Accessed (March 5, 2025). https://100.best-poems.net/dash.html

ACKNOWLEDGEMENTS

Writing this book has been a journey shaped by the support, insights, and encouragement of many individuals along the way. I'm incredibly grateful for the people who contributed their time, wisdom, and unwavering belief in my work!

To my husband and boys, your patience and understanding during long writing sessions and countless brainstorming conversations made this possible. Thank you for being my biggest cheerleaders!

To my assistant, your keen eye, thoughtful feedback, and commitment to elevating this work helped turn ideas into a polished manuscript. Your partnership has been invaluable!

To the leaders I've had the privilege of working with, thank you for trusting me to walk alongside you in your professional journeys. Your stories, challenges, and breakthroughs inspired many of the insights shared within these pages!

To my close friends and mentors — you know who you are — thank you for asking tough questions, offering candid advice, and reminding me to celebrate progress along the way!

Finally, to you — the reader — thank you for your curiosity, your willingness to rethink how you approach your capacity, and your commitment to evolving both yourself and your organization. Your desire to lead with intention fuels my passion for this work!

With gratitude for the exceptional people who shape my work,
Hilani

ABOUT AUTHOR

Hilani Ellis, Founder of Exceptional Executives and Exceptional Admins—two talent acquisition and development companies—is recognized as a Capacity Architect, a trusted partner to professionals seeking greater productivity without compromise. She sheds light on how remodeling work styles expands capacity and strengthens performance. As a sought-after advisor and facilitator, Hilani has directly impacted over 400 teams, from fast-growing startups to established enterprises. In every engagement, she delivers tailored strategies and insights drawn from more than 45,000 hours of research and real-world experience.

Leaders and professionals who embrace her strategies consistently expand their capacity, allowing them to focus on high-value initiatives, resulting in accelerated business growth and greater fulfillment in their work.

Hilani welcomes connections and conversations about leadership, capacity, and evolving work styles. To learn more, visit www.HilaniEllis.com or follow her on https://www.linkedin.com/in/hilaniellis/.

Learn more about Hilani at www.HilaniEllis.com/meet-me

www.ingramcontent.com/pod-product-compliance
Lightning Source LLC
Chambersburg PA
CBHW020937090426
42736CB00010B/1171